The foundational book in the *Leading For Change Guided Workbook Series*

BUILD YOUR MODEL FOR LEADING CHANGE

A guided workbook to catalyze clarity and confidence in leading yourself and others

By Marsha Acker

TeamCatapult Publishing

978-1-7356554-2-0

Cover Design/Illustrations/Interior Design: Alex Thomas

Printed in the United States of America

For Sarah Hill and Tony Melville

With deep appreciation and gratitude for rocking my world with the concept of model building many years ago and for continuously modelling generosity, kindness, and constraint.

CONTENTS

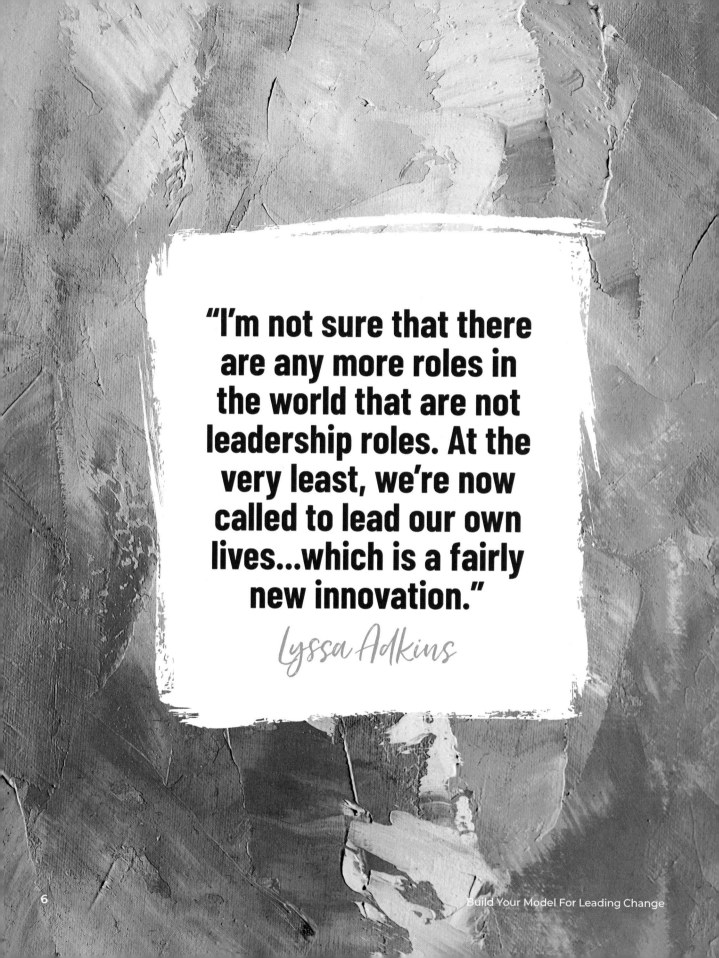

"I'm not sure that there are any more roles in the world that are not leadership roles. At the very least, we're now called to lead our own lives...which is a fairly new innovation."

Lyssa Adkins

Welcome!

INTRODUCTION

If you've picked up this workbook, chances are you're thinking about leadership and change — whether it's how to lead yourself, how to lead change, or how to respond to the changes happening all around you.

You are not alone.

Of course, leadership comes in many different forms and styles, and it can easily feel like the change we're not expecting is the one we get. And when it comes to change, perhaps the only certainty is that it is continuous — the individuals and systems we interact with on a daily basis are constantly changing.

In other words, part of the core work of becoming leaders who are prepared and truly able to lead change is to increase our awareness of what's happening — in ourselves, in our teams, in our group dynamics — so that we can be intentional about our choices and can create the impact we intend.

What you'll discover in this book is that when it comes to building a model for leading change, the first step is to explore the intersection of three core models: your behavioral model, your model for leadership, and your model for living. Without these three models defined and refined, your capacity for leading change will never reach its full potential.

This foundational book in the Leading for Change Workbook Series is designed to launch you on a path of model-building that will catalyze your clarity and your confidence so that you can begin to lead change with skill, courage, and a strong understanding of who you are.

WHAT IS CHANGE?

When you think about leading change, what is it, exactly, that you're wanting to lead? And how do you intend to go about doing it?

We tend to think about change when we want something different than what we've been getting. And because we're human, we will often articulate the change we want through the lens of our own behavioral preferences. After all, that's how we see the world. We usually want to see behavioral change that reflects the behaviors we believe in.

If we are at point A and we want to get to point B (or point C, D, or Z) and there is a gap between where we are and where we want to be — well, something has to change, doesn't it? When we think about change, we're often imagining what it would be like to live in a world where we have closed the gap.

But how do we actually get there?

- If you're in charge of leading a team toward the desired change, what do you actually do?

- If you're not in a position where you are in charge but have still been tasked with making change happen, what do you do from the seat you're in?

Often, when leaders need something done in a hurry and don't feel like they have time for people to get on board, they just tell their team what to do and expect compliance with the instructions provided. Well, that can certainly bring about a sense of change — but what's really been achieved is compliance, and it's temporary. It won't last. And about the only thing we will collectively learn from compliance is how to comply with the instructions and how to complain to our friends about the compliance later on.

Getting other people to implement a change in a meaningful, sustainable way can feel like an elusive, sometimes never-ending quest. But it's not impossible. Not at all.

To lead change — to really lead change — we need to shift the how. We need a clearer, actionable understanding of how to lead change. And it doesn't happen by changing others — in fact, we can all agree that it's impossible to change other people. How we lead change is by creating the conditions that make change possible — the conditions that make change happen.

Sure, there are barriers we all know exist. But the biggest barrier to change — the real problem — is that we block what we already have. We block what we need to bring about change in ourselves, in our teams, and in our organizations by blocking our collective access to the knowledge we already have. Why? Because we haven't learned to understand and address the daily breakdowns that happen on the level of human interaction and conversation.

In order to lead change, we need leaders who are interventionists — individuals who have developed the skills to dissolve fragmentation, change the nature and quality of conversations, and unlock the collective wisdom of the group by prioritizing a deeper understanding of human behavior — including our own.

Because all change starts on the level of individual and group behavior.

So, how does behavior change happen? It starts with the ability to have effective conversations — conversations in which all parties feel heard and seen and that unfold in a way that enables people to say what they really think. Effective conversations create space for different points of view, balance the skills of inquiry and advocacy, and facilitate participants' ability to learn and maybe even shift their thinking, beliefs, or mindset.

As humans, we all tend to think we know how to hold a conversation. After all, we do it every day, right? But skillful conversations of the sort that can really shift team culture and facilitate organizational change initiatives require so much more of us. They require us to look within, to learn new behavioral skills and awareness, and be able to trace the patterns of human interaction with a developed level of competency.

Then — and only then — can we unlock the power of leading change. Through the skills of behavioral competency and conversational awareness, you will be able to unlock the collective intelligence that already exists in your organization.

Think of this workbook as your guided journey through the process.

- To start on this journey, you need to know yourself and your behavior. That starts with a functional level of awareness around your behavioral model.

- The second step is to develop your model for leadership. How do you orient toward others? What does leadership mean to you? What are you trying to change?

- The next step is to explore and define your model for living by asking yourself for honest insight into what meaningful balance in work and life looks like for you.

- And, then, finally, you will be prepared to build a model for leading change that can lead you forward sustainably and impactfully.

The four models addressed in this workbook — and the journey you will take to define them for yourself — will give you a foundation for leading sustainable behavior change no matter what your starting point is.

Warning: this is not a weekend study project. It's a lifetime journey, should you choose to accept it. But it doesn't need to take you a lifetime to get your feet under you! This workbook is designed to help you develop a functional level of self-awareness, an actionable understanding of how you interact with others, a clear vision about the kind of change you want to effect, and the skills to identify what kinds of conversations are needed in order to lead change — starting now.

DEFINING YOUR MODEL FOR LEADING CHANGE

Did you know that you already have a model for leading change? We all do, but what few of us do is actually define it for ourselves. Very few of us take the time and energy to understand, clarify, and identify for ourselves and others what our model for leading change looks like. But doing this work is where the good stuff happens.

The very act of getting clear about what's in your model for leading change clarifies (for you and for others) why you're doing what you're doing.

Throughout this text, you will see me use the words "leader" and "leadership." Let me be clear: I'm referring to <u>you</u> and how you show up. Lyssa Adkins said it well when speaking with me on my podcast. She said, "I'm not sure there are any more roles in the world that are not leadership roles. At the very least, we're now called to lead our own lives...which is a fairly new innovation."

Regardless of our role on a team or in the organization, we all have leadership to bring, and we all have the ability to be a leader in every moment.

But it requires us to adapt our mental models of leadership.

- Leaders can come from anywhere — not just the top

- Leadership can take on many different forms — not just being the first to make a move

Leadership can look like being the first follower, it can look like supporting and championing the ideas of others, and it can look like sensing what's needed in the moment and responding accordingly. It can also look like leading together with others, sharing leadership.

Learning to let leadership take all these different forms is what I call having Leadership Range.

In her book *Daring to Lead*, Brene Brown defines a leader as "anyone who takes responsibility for finding the potential in people and processes, and who has the courage to develop that potential." We all take on many different roles — and therefore behaviors and actions — in any given moment. Even a leader who has positional authority in an organization should develop range in their leadership. They need the ability to step

THIS WORKBOOK IS FOR YOU

It can be hard to step into the realm of humility and vulnerability — which are at the heart of working effectively with others to lead sustainable, meaningful change.

This workbook is for you if you are struggling with...

- A leadership role that is stretching you beyond your current capabilities and you're not sure what you need to do next

- A team that wants change or an organization that wants change for a team — and you've been tasked to make it happen

- A team stuck in conflict

- A personal or professional relationship that is stuck or unproductive

In other words, I've designed this guided workbook for you.

I've designed it to be a resource to catalyze a journey of personal growth with a direct impact on your ability to successfully lead yourself and others and be clear about how change happens.

Stick with the guided process laid out in this workbook, and by the end you will:

- Have a clear understanding of how your personal behavioral model and your leadership model are inextricably linked

- See how leading change is intertwined with every aspect of our lives

- Understand that clarity comes from being very specific and intentional about what we are trying to change and how we believe change happens

- See what's involved in leadership and leading change from a process and behavioral lens

- Have clarity about where you want to grow and what's not for you

- Have started to define your behavioral model, your model for leadership, and your model for living

forward and they need the ability to step back — to make space for others to put forward ideas and to engage meaningfully with change.

We all own our part and are responsible for the experiences we generate. Likewise, we are all constrained by the systems we live and work in — politics, culture, different models of leadership, biases, etc. Our work is to be clear about how we behave and how we lead — understanding why we do what we do and what impact we are having on those around us.

From this work will come clarity and grounded confidence for how we can creatively navigate our lives— with range, with intention, and with courage.

No matter what role you play in your organization or where you are in your life and career, there is some aspect of the work you do that contributes to a greater purpose and a greater good. This book is designed to help you tap into that purpose with clarity and self-awareness.

STRUCTURAL DYNAMICS

Throughout this workbook, I'll be sharing with you extensively from the model I've found fundamental in understanding myself and informing my work with leaders and teams: Structural Dynamics.

Structural Dynamics is a theory founded by a researcher named David Kantor. It illuminates communication patterns, behaviors, and dynamics in a way that makes them plain to see, easy to name, and therefore possible to work with and improve.

This workbook extends the process of model-building that Kantor defined in his book *Reading the Room* by offering a guided-thinking and reflective-journaling process designed to help you discover and define your model for leading change.

If you haven't read *Reading the Room* already, I encourage you to pick it up! It has been profoundly impactful in my own work and life. However, you do not need to have read it to use this workbook. You will engage with Kantor's ideas and guidance as a means of model-building, but through the lens of the work I've been doing with leaders and teams for over a decade.

Over time, like any practitioner, I've blended the thinking and the work of many wonderful colleagues to form the basis of how I coach and train others. If you dive into the references section at the end of this workbook (and I hope you do!) you will find a treasure trove of useful texts to help deepen your journey as a leader and a human.

My hope is that there's something for everyone here: some learning, some journaling, and some real-life examples of models in action. But the core of this powerful workbook is in the guided journaling that makes up the majority of the pages to come.

Everyone needs
A THINKING PARTNER...

Thinking partners are great.

The right thinking partner might see things a bit differently than you do and they might have different models that they use. These differences can not only spur new thinking around your model(s), they can inspire questions that will illuminate the holes or gaps.

I think everyone should have at least one thinking partner in their model-building journey. Even better to have a small group! But if this is new territory for you, one is the perfect start.

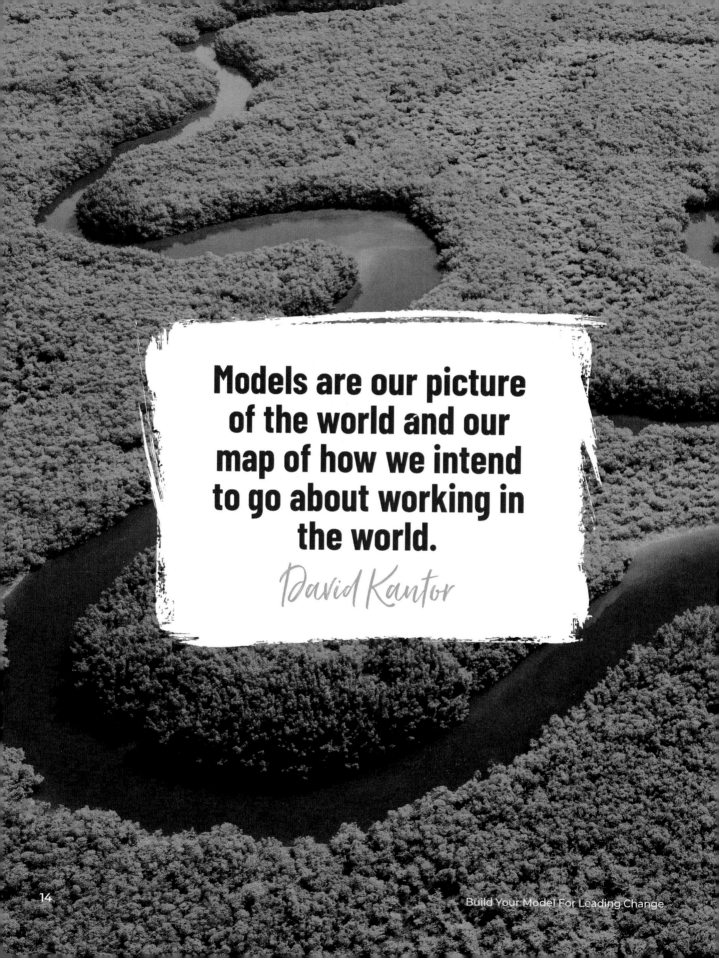

Models are our picture of the world and our map of how we intend to go about working in the world.

David Kantor

Models: Bringing clarity and confidence to a complex and ever-evolving world

The journey you are embarking on in this guided workbook is one of self-awareness so that you can expand your skills and capacity, and so that you can feel ready to step confidently into the space of leading change.

This is the critical first step.

This workbook starts from the premise that in order to build a model for leading change, we all need to develop three kinds of foundational models for ourselves: a behavioral model, a leadership model, and a model for living. For those of you familiar with David Kantor's work, you will likely be familiar with his belief that we all need a personal model, a professional model, and a model for living. But, because of its focus on leading change, this workbook explores a more precise intersection.

Your model for leading change sits at the intersection of your core patterns and understanding of behavior, your core beliefs about leadership, and your core beliefs about living. By delving deeply into these key frameworks, developing your self-awareness, and taking the time to clarify — for yourself and others — how you understand and navigate competing ideas and interactions, you will be better prepared to create sustainable change for yourself, your team, and your organization.

The world around us is only getting more complex. Things are shifting and changing around us at enormous speed. By spending the time and energy to move thoughtfully through the pages of this workbook, you are laying the groundwork to show up with more confidence and greater clarity at every step along your path — no matter where the journey takes you.

So what is a model?

Models guide how we think about, make sense of, and take action in the world around us — and it all starts with a deep understanding and awareness of ourselves.

Deep knowing of self allows us to be more in command of our actions so that we may take more effective actions. Understanding our behavioral model is thus the foundational step for building models around how we work and how we live.

A behavioral model is simply a means of understanding how we process the events happening around us through the lens of our inner stories and understanding how we behave in any given circumstance. Developing our understanding of our behavioral models (why we do what we do) not only helps deepen our self-awareness, it expands the range of actions we feel like we have available to us in the moment. This is the focus of **Chapters 1 and 2**.

Chapter 3 of this workbook then turns to the process of building new models, and the process that then gets put into practice in **Chapter 4**, which delves into your model for leadership. We can define many professional models, but I would submit that the foundation to all models starts with how we view leadership and how change happens for ourselves and others. Our model for leadership is the foundation on which all other professional models will be built. In other words, a model for leadership is a way of starting with yourself so that you can engage effectively with others. It's deeply understanding how you can create (or not create) the space where change can happen.

Chapter 5 then turns toward using the model-building skills you've developed in **Chapters 3 and 4** to explore your model for living. A core part of defining a model for leadership (or any professional model), is defining your model for living. A model for living strives to answer critical questions like:

- "How shall I live?"

- "What is my purpose?"

- "What do I believe about life, leadership, and love?"

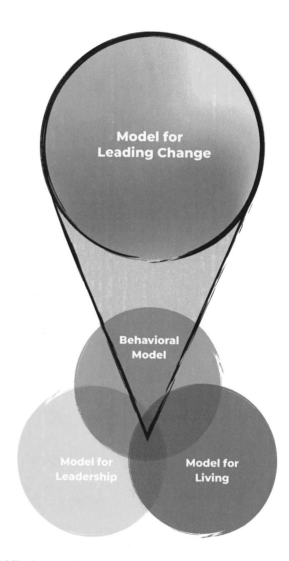

While the graphic above captures the relationship between the models explored in this workbook, there are an endless number of models you can build from here. On the opposite page is an example of just a few of the models I personally have spent time defining for myself.

This workbook concludes, therefore, by exploring this deep and impactful space.

Finally, **Chapter 6** bulids on everything you've learned about model-building so far to help you build a realistic, effective, and personal model for leading change.

AN EXAMPLE OF MY MODELS

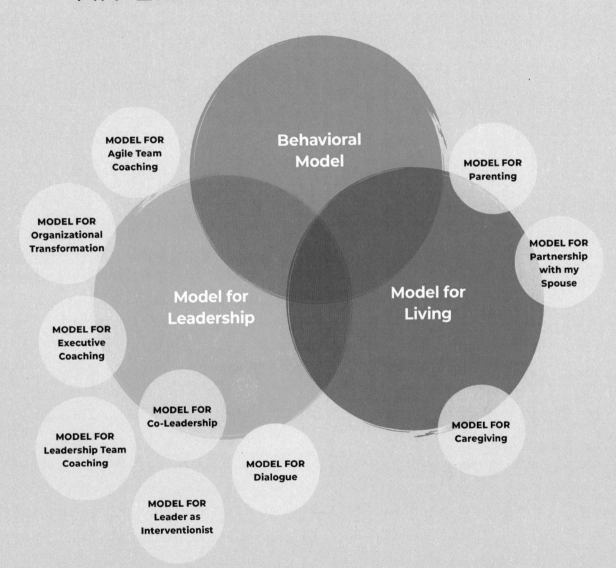

MODEL FOR
Agile Team
Coaching

MODEL FOR
Organizational
Transformation

MODEL FOR
Executive
Coaching

MODEL FOR
Leadership Team
Coaching

MODEL FOR
Co-Leadership

MODEL FOR
Leader as
Interventionist

MODEL FOR
Dialogue

Behavioral
Model

MODEL FOR
Parenting

MODEL FOR
Partnership
with my
Spouse

Model for
Leadership

Model for
Living

MODEL FOR
Caregiving

As you can tell, it's easy to spend a lifetime deepening our self-awareness, defining our approach, and generally refining our understanding of who we are and how we show up through the process of model-building. And I believe that there is no better use of one's time.

"The thing always happens that you really believe in; and the belief in a thing makes it happen."

Frank Lloyd Wright

THE IMPORTANCE OF ARTICULATING OUR OWN MODEL

If we are going to lead change in a meaningful and effective way, we need our own models to guide us.

When there's a difficult task in front of you or a long road to haul, it can be tempting to just keep researching and collecting ideas, hoping to glean something usable along the way. But when you only go an inch deep and a mile wide, it's easy to lose your internal compass and sense of purpose when faced with the complexity of human interaction. At some point, you'll want to be done researching and collecting ideas, and you'll likely decide it's time to deepen your awareness and develop your own approach and expertise.

Doing the work of developing your own model based on what works for you, what you feel deeply prepared for, your own experience, how you show up in your work, and what feels authentic is where clarity and confidence can show up. It's the first step in becoming self-authored versus other-authored.

What's the alternative to consciously engaging in model building?

Alice in Wonderland captures it perfectly in the following conversation with the Cheshire Cat:

"Would you tell me, please, which way I ought to go from here?"

"That depends a good deal on where you want to get to," said the Cat.

"I don't much care where—" said Alice.

"Then it doesn't matter which way you go," said the Cat.

"—so long as I get SOMEWHERE," Alice added as an explanation.

"Oh, you're sure to do that," said the Cat, "if you only walk long enough."

Models become our way of seeing our "truth."

Yet sometimes our truth can be different than someone else's truth. What happens then?

Chances are, this is where conflict and debate will emerge. But when you have clarity in your model and you are able to articulate it, you can not only weather conflict, you can harness its productive potential.

If I am clear and grounded in my model and I can describe it in a way that you can see it — and if you can describe your model in a way that I can see it — then we can engage in a conversation about our models as objects. We can both step into the realm of curiosity. We can be curious about the assumptions that we are each making, and we can describe what we see and what informs our thinking.

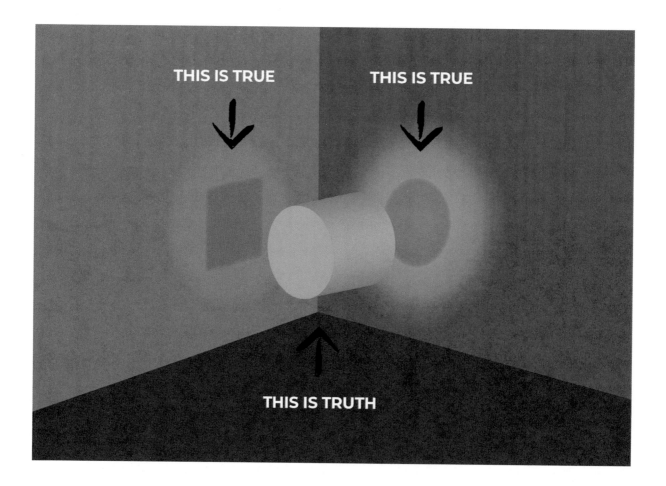

In other words, being clear about my model allows me to be grounded and curious about yours.

I don't feel the need to make you wrong in order for me to be right.

I can see that there is more than one way of looking at a problem or situation.

I can accept that different approaches can work just as well as — and maybe even better than — mine.

As a result of this kind of curiosity, we may shift our thinking and expand our model, or we may simply expand our awareness and understanding of others. Either one is a win, especially because the process increases our tolerance for difference.

But in order for us to engage in a cross-model conversation, we both need to be able to articulate our model in a way that is accessible to us and others. And that's why this workbook exists — it's a place to get started and record your thinking and reflections.

It's a space for you to move through the work of developing, refining, and learning to articulate your own model — for yourself and for leading change.

JOURNALING AS A REFLECTIVE PRACTICE

When I ask leaders if they have a journaling practice, their answers vary. Some say, "I've tried, but I don't get it. I'm not sure I'm doing it right." Others say they're not sure why it's important or what they're supposed to get from it. And some say, "Yes! I journal every day and I find it really helpful." So, wherever you currently fall on this spectrum, you are not alone.

If you already have a practice that's working for you, great! Feel free to move to the next section of this workbook! But if you don't have a consistent practice, stay here with me and let's unpack the practice of journaling as a core practice of developing and deepening your personal behavioral model, your model for leadership, and your model for living.

Reflection is a critical part of the model building we discussed in the last section. After all, how can you really know what's working for you and what's not if you don't take the time to think about it — honestly, openly, and with curiosity? Whether you are in the phase of Imitation, Constraint, or Autonomy, your reflective journaling practice is the place where a lot of the deep work happens.

Throughout this guided workbook, you will be led through specific prompts to help you reflect on yourself, your beliefs, your stories, and your values. These will help you get going in your practice while guiding you through a journey to develop your leadership model. But a strong journaling practice can last a lifetime if you simply commit to building on the foundation I'm introducing here.

I used to be that person who didn't find journaling helpful. But then I learned to let go of "doing it right" and just simply let my brain talk to me through my pen. Continue reading for some helpful tips and guidance to get you started in your practice.

Remember: you can't get it wrong, and getting started is better than not starting at all.

You don't have to see the whole staircase... just take the first step.

Martin Luther King Jr.

Developing a personal reflective practice

Reflection can occur before, during, and after an event. In each stage, different kinds of learning happen.

According to Donald Schon, a reflective practice can take two forms:

- Reflection in action
- Reflection on action

Reflection in action happens during the activity you are engaged in. It is a process of taking the view from the balcony, observing your action(s), and adapting in the moment according to what's happening.

Things to consider:

- What are your thoughts in this moment?
- How are you feeling?
- What's resonant for you?
- What, if anything, is causing you hesitation?

Reflection on action happens after the activity has ended and is based on what you remember from the situation.

Things to consider:

- What was the activity/event like for you?
- What were you feeling?
- What were you thinking?
- What was hard?
- What was easy?
- What are you noticing about yourself now?
- What are you learning?

While these two forms of reflection are incredibly powerful, I would add a third: reflecting before action.

Reflecting before action allows you to reflect with the specific purpose of setting your intention about how you want to show up in the activity or event to come.

Things to consider:

- What's your ideal outcome?
- How do you want to show up?
- Who do you want to be?
- What might be hard or challenging?
- How do you want to be when it gets hard?
- What kind of leader do you want to be?

If you're new to the process of reflection, start by reflecting on action first. It's easier to look back and think through what happened than it is to reflect in the moment. If, however, you have come to this guided workbook already practiced in the art of reflection, then by all means start by reflecting before action, then in action, and finally on action. The idea here is to start where you are and build on your reflection skills so that you can steadily deepen your practice

HOW TO GET STARTED

Keep a reflective journal

First and foremost, if you're going to start a journaling practice, you need a place to reflect! Neuroscientific research has shown that our brains, health, and well-being benefit from journaling with pen and paper. If you're inclined, treat yourself to a brand new hardcover journal that is dedicated to your reflective journaling on leadership and change. Enjoy the feel of it!

But if pen and paper are not for you, then start writing where you are most drawn to. Don't let the mechanics keep you from starting.

Make it a habit

Reflective journaling will have the greatest impact on your ability to read yourself and navigate groups when you reflect daily. Have a Space, a Place, and a Time. Make it a habit that you build into your life.

How to keep going

If the key step is to get started, the core benefits come from staying the path. This is about creating a practice, sticking with it, and aiming for progress over perfection.

But when we talk about making Space, Place, and Time, it's not always easy! It requires intention and dedication.

Daily reflection practices are often inhibited by:

A lack of time – With work, our home life, our hobbies, and everything else on our plate, it can feel hard to prioritize a reflective practice.

The new-ness of it – Staring at a blank page can be intimidating. You might be thinking, "I've never done this before, what if I don't do it 'right'?"

Motivation – Like any new habit, doubt about the outcome might creep in and decrease your motivation. You might be wondering if this will really be helpful. You might think, "It would be easier if I could just look up a tool or a new model to help me instead."

Fear – This is a big one, especially as we deepen our reflection. Through this process, we're taking a long, honest assessment of ourselves, our behaviors, and our actions. You might be thinking, "I'm not sure I want to look deeply at myself, I'm afraid of what I might find."

Let me offer some hints and tips to help you get the most of your practice and really stick with it.

- You can't get it wrong!

- Find an accountability partner.

- Give it time. It takes practice to make journaling part of your daily habit, and it takes consistency to help you catch sight of your own behaviors.

- No shaming! Even if we don't like something about ourselves (and hint: we all have shadows and darker sides), the less we look at them or the more we try to ignore them, the bigger they become. So be easy, kind, and gentle. Look through this lens: you behave the way you behave for a reason. Be curious about that reason and make the decision of whether you want to continue with the behavior or not.

- Start somewhere — and make it part of your daily routine. Even if it's just 10 minutes of your morning or a few minutes before bed, create a practice and strive for progress over perfection.

Build your reflective writing muscle

When we write about past events, it's common to look back and simply describe who, what, when, and where. This is descriptive writing. It's helpful, but only as a way to prompt your reflections.

Reflective writing is writing about your thoughts, feelings, why you did what you did, how you did it, and what you might do in the future. This means it's best if you keep reflective writing in the first person ("I" statements). After all, this is about YOU.

The next chart provides a useful example of descriptive writing versus reflective writing.

Descriptive Writing	Reflective Writing
We started off the meeting by waiting for Sam to show up. There were three of us in the room and the silence was awkward.	As I start to write my reflections about this meeting I'm really frustrated by how the meeting went yesterday. It felt like such a waste of time and I was really confused at the end about what I am supposed to do next.
When Sam arrived 15 minutes late we were forced to skip the introductions and move right to the agenda.	As I was waiting for the meeting to start with three others in the room, it felt so awkward to me. I didn't know them or why they were there. As I write this I'm aware that I made some assumptions about the purpose of the meeting and who would be there.
Then someone else introduced a new topic that derailed the conversation.	I know Sam to be someone who is very reliable and timely, and I also assumed the meeting would start on time.
We never got to the topic that I thought we were going to talk about, and I left feeling so angry about having wasted my time.	I'm realizing now that there must have been some reason for why Sam was so late. I'm also aware that without a clear purpose I'm not sure why everyone else was at the meeting. I just assumed we were all there for the same purpose.
	Upon reflection there are two things that I'm taking away:
	• Follow up with Sam to see what might have been the cause for the delayed start
	• In the future, I'll be clear about the purpose of the meeting and the agenda before agreeing to attend

A strong journaling and reflection practice will sustain you well beyond the pages of this workbook and any of the upcoming workbooks in this series. It is a practice that is for you and you alone — but everyone around you will benefit from your work.

So go treat yourself to a journal! Make it something that you will be drawn to each day.

DON'T SHY AWAY FROM THE MESSINESS

Leadership is being in the mess and being comfortable with being uncomfortable.

In fact, I think the leaders that have the greatest following and the greatest number of people who would refer to them as being someone with a significant and memorable impact on others (in a positive way) are those leaders who are willing to show up as human beings in the moment.

They are real, authentic, curious, scared, afraid, sad, remorseful, excited, happy, and joyful. They are someone who is willing to have — and be with others who have — a full range of emotions.

It's fatiguing to be around others who are pretending to be something or someone they're not. And let's be honest, it's fatiguing to pretend you are someone who you're not. When we show up inauthentically, it creates a ripple effect where everyone around us begins to pretend, defend, and deflect.

I am so passionate about the humanness of leadership that I've devoted an entire podcast to it. It's called *Defining Moments of Leadership*: Inspiring stories and tangible lessons from leaders growing their leadership range, clarifying and refining their model for leadership and daring to define a moment rather than let a moment define them. If you haven't had a chance to tune in, I invite you to join me there. It really is eye-opening and inspiring.

I would be willing to bet that every person on the podcast has done their work around their model for leadership. If you really listen to the words my guests use and the stories they tell, you will hear their model come through loud and clear.

Quotes from Leaders	What it says about their model for leadership
"I value curiosity and I know I don't have all the answers."	Curiosity is a value. I assume that I don't have all the answers and I'm okay with that — even if others are not — and I trust in the process of uncovering the answers with others through the act of being curious.
"It's my job to help others be successful."	I believe that my success is defined by creating an environment and the conditions for others to be successful.
"The political capital you hold in an organization is not just to be spent on maximizing your career, it's also to maximize the work of others — even if that means taking a personal risk."	My focus in my leadership is on the whole system, not just myself or other individuals. Our success comes from looking systemically. It's scary to take a personal risk, but I believe it's my role to do that, especially if I have the political capital to possibly make a difference for others and our customers.

These statements all reflect self-knowledge that these leaders have developed through deep self-awareness – they have refined a model for understanding themselves in relation to others and the world around them. They know why they do what they do.

A brilliant term coined by Brene Brown is "**grounded confidence**," it's that sense of calm clarity that comes from a deep knowing of self. It comes from knowing how you want to show up when things get really tough (your behavior model) and having a way to see and make sense of what's happening around you (your model of leading change). Having these models allows you to step forward into muddy and uncertain spaces confident that while you don't have the answers, you can trust in the process of discovering the answers.

Grounded confidence is the space of clarity, the space of awareness, and the space of true leadership. And it starts with defining and refining your core models, even if it's a messy process.

Here's my promise to you: getting started is far more important than having it all figured out.

Developing your model for leading change is a process of continuous self-assessment, deep self-awareness, and cultivating new mindsets. And ultimately it's about being able to build an environment where all players can address complexity with creativity and openness. It won't happen overnight, but it will happen.

Don't worry, you've got this.

NOTES

We develop knowledge of self . . .

so that we can give up the self and serve others.

CHAPTER 1

Understanding
Our Behavior:
The Structures
and Dynamics of
Communication

AWARENESS PRECEDES CHOICE PRECEDES CHANGE

Whether you are here because you feel called to build a model for leadership or because you recognize the importance of having a leadership model to lead change effectively, your first port of call along the journey is here: understanding and developing your behavioral model — a lens consciously developed through self-awareness that informs how we see everything.

How do you behave in the moment and why? This is your foundation.

A behavioral model starts with awareness.

Awareness is being able to clearly see yourself in action and understand the causality — how your actions impact others, how and why the actions of others impact you, and what you can do about it. It is also about growing your tolerance for behavior that is different from our own.

Choice is about taking a different action, one that is in alignment with your intent.

Change is about bringing something new to life.

While many of us create models for business processes and roadmaps to scale improvements, few of us formally engage in a process of intentional model building for ourselves. Yet it's the one thing that has the ability to create greater clarity, confidence, enjoyment, and success in leading change.

Deeply knowing, expanding, and being more in command of our behavioral model is our ongoing life's work, one that is never really done. But it's through this process that we can make change happen for ourselves and improve our own performance, our team's performance, and our entire organization.

Developing your personal behavioral model is the foundation for building your model for leadership. And it all starts with YOU.

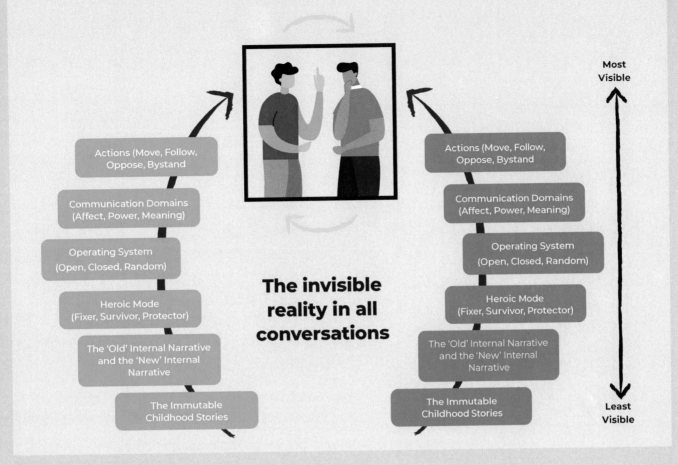

The invisible reality in all conversations

Most Visible → Least Visible

Actions (Move, Follow, Oppose, Bystand

Communication Domains (Affect, Power, Meaning)

Operating System (Open, Closed, Random)

Heroic Mode (Fixer, Survivor, Protector)

The 'Old' Internal Narrative and the 'New' Internal Narrative

The Immutable Childhood Stories

As we discussed in the opening section on model building, there are many theories and models of behavior. You may have several models or assessments that you already engage with to help you become more aware of yourself, especially in terms of how you interact with others.

In this workbook, we will be using the theory of Structural Dynamics developed by David Kantor to create the framework for understanding your behavioral model. Kantor originally developed this theory during his tenure as a clinical psychologist at Harvard University. Then, through his work with MIT and the Dialogue Project, he further developed it to apply to organizational theory and leadership model building.

I have found Structural Dynamics to be the most comprehensive and universally applicable model for understanding and making sense of the dynamics of communication — making the invisible structures in our daily behavior more visible. It provides a clear, neutral language that you can use to name the various structures that show up in both individual and group dynamics. As you continue developing your self-awareness, this clarity and specificity will allow you to develop the ability to see what actions you might take in the moment and understand the impact you have in the room.

So, in this section, I offer a concise breakdown of structural dynamics — along with key reflection prompts — to ground your understanding of this powerful framework. It will then become the backbone of discovering your personal behavioral model in the next section.

If you are interested in learning more about Structural Dynamics, I highly encourage you to pick up a copy of David Kantor's *Reading the Room*.

STRUCTURAL DYNAMICS AND THE ONGOING WORK OF SELF-AWARENESS

 According to Kari McLeod, having Structural Dynamics inform her personal behavioral model has given her a much deeper sense of herself, her relationships, and her work in the world.

"One of the biggest shifts for me has been to use Structural Dynamics as a lens through which I can view all sorts of interactions," she shares. "It gives me a chance to step away from the Moral Story and into the Structural Story."

Prior to developing her personal behavioral model, she describes herself as being quite reactive when she didn't agree with what was being said. Sometimes she would lash out with a barb, sometimes she would grow very quiet, and in particularly contentious interactions she would even storm off. In other circumstances, she found herself in a recurring pattern where she wouldn't articulate things that bothered her. She would do this in an attempt to preserve relationships.

"I would just sweep things under the rug. And the rug would get higher and higher as I swept more things under it. Ultimately, what would happen is the rug couldn't hold the contents, and one small thing would lead to a big blow up. It was never pretty. And the irony was that the thing I was doing to preserve the relationship, damaged the relationship."

Through the work of engaging Structural Dynamics and developing her personal behavioral model, Kari feels that she has more empathy for other people, more facility with how she communicates, and a deeper understanding of herself. But she'll be the first to tell you that it's an ongoing process.

"I think the most challenging part of model building is that having a personal model lets me see and be in the world in a different way, and at the same time, I have old patterns of seeing and being that have been with me for years. It can be frustrating to fall back into old patterns."

Kari McLeod

THE 4 LEVELS OF BEHAVIOR

Structural Dynamics consists of four connected levels of structure that help us understand behavior in the moment.

By looking at the structure of behaviors, we can make sense of what's happening in the moment and develop a language for naming what's happening. Doing so allows us to see where we are moving forward productively in the conversation and when we might be stuck or ineffective in the conversation.

Structural dynamics asserts that the structure of our conversations determines the performance of our conversations.

Just like the structure of a riverbed determines the flow of water — whether it flows fast or slow, smooth or choppy — the structure of conversations determines their outcomes. If a conversation is not effective, intervening in the structure serves to change the nature of the conversation — just like moving rocks around in the riverbed to change the flow of the water.

The gift of structural dynamics is that it does not label behavior into subjective terminology ("good behaviors"/"bad behaviors") or assign broad classifications. It's nuanced and specific to the various needs of full and productive conversations.

And it's based on the fact that we can code the conversation in the moment and objectively understand the actions that are occurring (and thus what is happening in the conversation) in real time.

The 4 levels of behavior are:

Level 1: Action Modes — These are the four kinds of conversational actions (speech acts) that exist in all of our communication

Level 2: Operating Systems — These are the three types of systems that create our implicit rules for how we behave and converse with one another

Level 3: Communication Domains — These are the three types of language that we use to convey what matters or what's important to us

Level 4: Childhood Stories — These are the experiences we had growing up that lay down the stories that inform how we interact with the world today

STRUCTURAL DYNAMICS:
Four Levels for Coding Behavior

**Level 1:
Action
Modes**

MOVE   OPPOSE   BYSTAND   FOLLOW

**Level 2:
Operating
Systems**

OPEN   CLOSED   RANDOM

**Level 3:
Communication
Domains**

POWER   AFFECT   MEANING

**Level 4:
Childhood
Stories**

FORMATIVE
EXPERIENCES   OLD INTERNAL
NARRATIVE   NEW INTERNAL
NARRATIVE

Build Your Model For Leading Change

NOTES

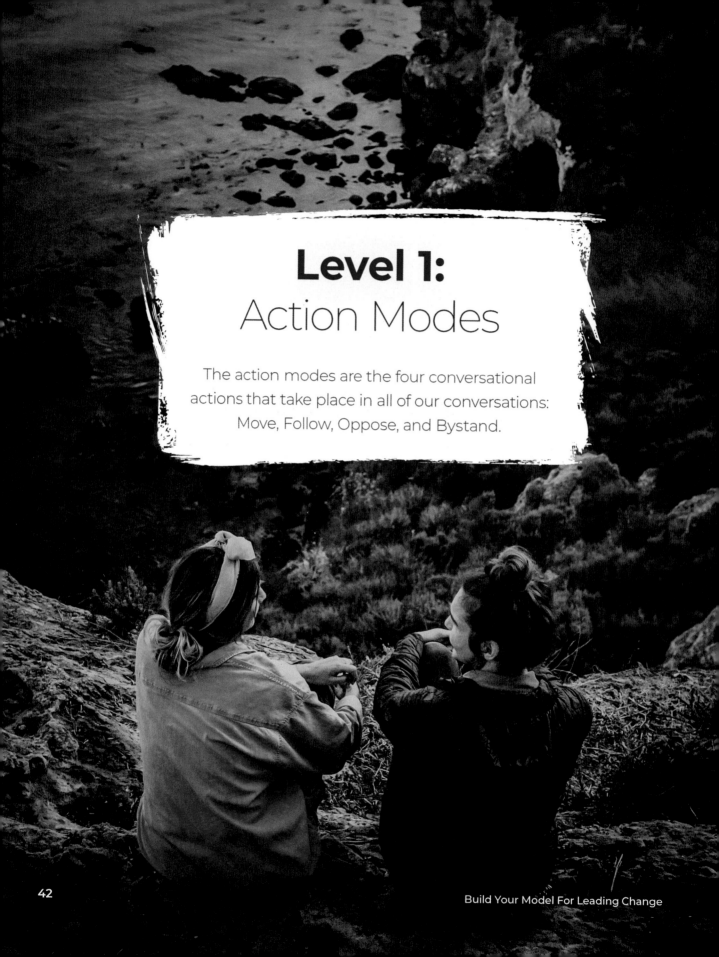

Level 1:
Action Modes

The action modes are the four conversational actions that take place in all of our conversations: Move, Follow, Oppose, and Bystand.

Every sentence or phrase we say can be coded into one of these four actions, called "speech acts." In order for the conversation to be effective, we need all four of them to be voiced and active. When one or more of them is missing, the conversation can become stuck.

As individuals, we will have two or three actions that we voice often and one or two actions that we use less frequently. The context matters, so who you're talking to and the situation you're in can change your behavior.

MOVE

Move sets the initial direction in a conversation.

For example: "In this meeting, let's talk about the new product launch date."

FOLLOW

Follow supports or finishes the direction. It gets behind an idea and carries it forward to completion.

For example: "I agree, I think we need to define the launch date soon. We're getting very tight on time."

OPPOSE

Oppose challenges or offers correction by providing alternatives.

For example: "I disagree that we're getting tight on time. We still have three more weeks to make the decision on the launch date."

BYSTAND

Bystand offers a morally neutral perspective by observing and naming what's happening, bridging ideas, or inquiring about someone else's idea.

For example: "We have two different points of view about the timeline. From your perspective, what's tight about the time right now?*

ACTION MODES SELF-ASSESSMENT

Based on nearly a decade of experience as a coach, instructor and mentor, here's what I've come to believe: in order to make sense of behaviors in the moment, it's really helpful to have a model that helps you see and name the specific actions taken and that gives you a way of making sense of them.

In other words, a model helps you operate at a behavorial level and helps you to see how specific actions weave together to form bigger patterns.

Structural Dynamics does that. You may have other models that you'll return to after this, but for now, I recommend taking a baseline assessment that specifically addresses behavior in relation to the Level 1 Action Modes (Move, Follow, Oppose, Bystand).

Next up are two ways to get started. The first is a quick reflection exercise, the second is a powerful free assessment you can take online. There are also paid assessments you can take, but I recommend starting with what's readily available at no cost.

Go ahead and pause with the following two assessment models. Take both and take your time. These will form the basis for the deeper questions we'll tackle in the next section.

Action Modes Quick Self-Assessment

Think about a specific context or group scenario.

Move:

What percentage of your time do you spend putting forth new ideas or positions for others to consider?

_____%

Follow:

What percentage of your time do you spend offering support or following through on the ideas or positions put forth by others?

_____%

Bystand:

What percentage of your time do you spend inquiring about ideas or offering observations and perspectives that bridge competing ideas?

_____%

Oppose:

What percentage of your time do you spend challenging or enhancing ideas, positions, or proposed directions?

_____%

The bMaps behavioral map assessment

The bMaps assessment provides you with an understanding of your behavior at the Level 1 Actions (Move, Follow, Oppose, Bystand) in both low and high stakes. It is a great place to start and goes much deeper than the quick assessment on the previous page.

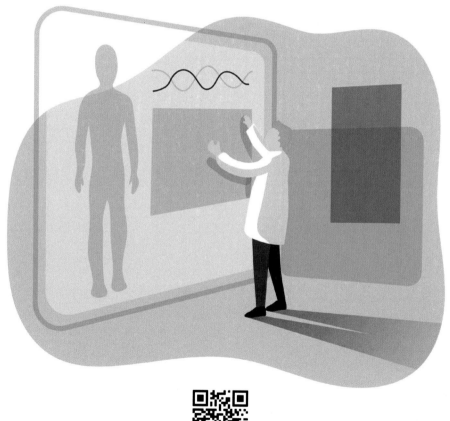

Take your free online assessment at https://trybmaps.com/en-us/

You may also take a paid version of the bMaps assessment at www.trybmaps.com. It covers all three levels of structural dynamics — Actions, Communication Domains ,and Operating Systems — in both low stakes and high stakes.

Build Your Model For Leading Change

Reflection Time

Now that you have taken these assessments, you have a basic snapshot of how the four Level 1 Action Modes (Move, Follow, Oppose, and Bystand) show up for you in conversations. All on its own, having this awareness will deepen your understanding of how you show up in the moment.

In this workbook, we take a particularly deep dive into Action Modes because — in my experience — they are the most visible speech act and the easiest to work with. I'll introduce you to the other levels of behavior in the following sections, but for now, we'll focus on the Action Modes so you can deepen your awareness through reflection and self-exploration.

Are you ready?

MOVE

Deepening Insights

- When do you find it easy to put forward ideas?

- What's the impact this has on others?

- In what contexts do you withhold your ideas?

- How often are you the first to speak?

- When you put forward an idea, do you offer places for others to also put forward ideas?

- Do you invite differing points of view?

While moves intend direction, commitment, and clarity, they are sometimes experienced as omnipotent, pushy, or dictatorial.

- Can you think of a time when you've had that impact on someone?

- What was happening?

- What was that like?

OPPOSE

Deepening Insights

- What's it like for you when you disagree with the direction a conversation is going? What do you do? Do you voice your disagreement, remain silent, or change the subject?

- If you remain silent, what has you do so?

- What's it like for you to clearly voice your point of view, even if it's opposing someone else's? In what situations is it easier? In what situations is it more difficult?

- Was there ever a time where you opposed someone and it had a negative impact or consequence?

- What's it like for you to be opposed — to have someone else disagree with your idea? How do you respond? Do you voice your reaction or remain silent? Do you defend your position or inquire into theirs?

- Do you see value in voicing push-back on ideas? Why or why not?

- Journal about a time when the action of Oppose was not welcomed. What was the situation? What was the emotion that it created for you? What part, if any, of this story stays with you today?

Oppose is valuable and intends correction, courage, and protection, but it can be experienced as critical, competitive, and contrary.

- Reflect on a time where you've had this impact on someone. What was happening?

- What was that like for you?

FOLLOW

Deepening Insights

- What's it like for you to voice support or build on the ideas of others?

- What's important for you about voicing support?

- When do you find it more difficult to voice support? What might be the reason behind this?

- Can you think of a time when you didn't voice support?

Follow is valuable and offers completion, follow-through, and continuity, but it can be perceived as placating, indecisive, or pliant.

Reflect on a time when you may have had this impact on others. What do you notice?

BYSTAND

Deepening Insights

Bystand is valuable in offering a neutral perspective or bridging what can appear to be competing ideas but it can be experienced as withdrawn, judgemental, or disinterested.

- Reflect on a time where you may have been seeing or thinking something but you withheld your voice and remained silent. What had you be silent?

- What would you like to have said?

- How might you say that now, as a neutral Bystand - without judgement?

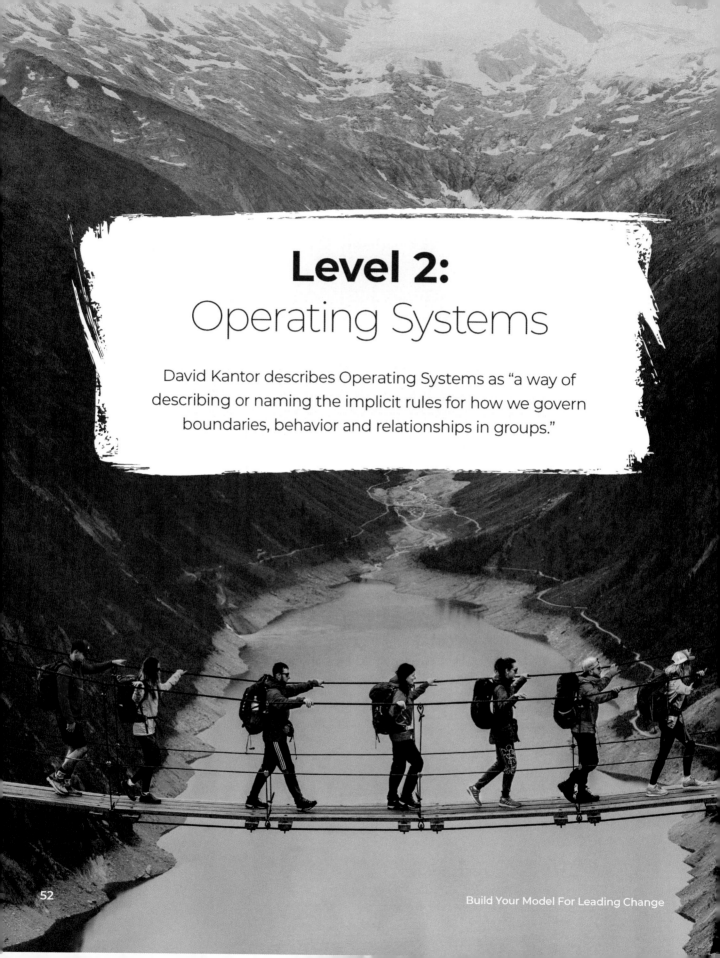

Level 2:
Operating Systems

David Kantor describes Operating Systems as "a way of describing or naming the implicit rules for how we govern boundaries, behavior and relationships in groups."

As with the Action Modes, every sentence we speak can be coded by listening to the implicit rules we articulate for how we want an action to be carried out — this is our Operating System. It reflects how we see the world — how we think things should unfold, how we think people should interact, whose voices we think should be heard in different contexts. And so our Operating System doesn't just affect the way we engage in conversations — it controls the speech of others, either by enabling or discouraging them from speaking.

There are three types of Operating Systems: open, closed, and random.

Stop! Before we continue into the definitions for these three types of Operating Systems, take a moment to jot down any judgements or immediate reactions you have to hearing the three labels ("open," "closed," "random"). Which of these three labels, if any, would you identify as "probably helpful" or "probably not helpful"? You may come back to these reflections in a moment...

Operating Systems help us make sense of group behavior at a systems level. All three types of Operating Systems need to be present in a high-functioning system, and each has value. Therefore, when one is overused, it comes at the cost of underutilizing another. This means that it is critical to understand YOUR preferred Operating System(s) so that you can learn to engage with others with greater awareness and recognize what implicit expectations and assumptions you are bringing into the dynamic.

So, for the purposes of this workbook, I'm going to introduce each kind of Operating System in more detail, focusing on how they can support your exploration of self and understand more fully which systems you personally prefer and why.

Open

 An open system places value on process, participation, and collaboration. In open system, we will value sharing authority and hearing from others. We will look to the collective group for making decisions by consensus.

Leadership in open systems will be based around what's good for the collective whole AND for the individual.

You might hear someone with a propensity for open system say, "It's important for us to hear every voice in this decision, since people will support what they help to create."

Open system intends to balance the good of the whole with the good of the individual, but when overused, open system can become dysfunctional. It can be experienced as "tyranny of process."

Closed

 A closed system emphasizes structure and planning, with value placed on tradition and hierarchy. In closed system, we will value the predictability of following the rules.

Leadership in closed systems manages for the good of the whole and finds clarity in roles, responsibilities, and processes.

Decision-making often comes from a central authority.

You might hear someone with a propensity for closed system say, *"A stable and orderly process is important."*

Closed system intends to manage for the good of the whole, but when overused, closed system can become dysfunctional. It can be experienced as "tyranny of tradition."

Random

Random system emphasizes innovation and values individual autonomy and creativity. There is a strong focus on individual preferences in a random system.

Leadership in random systems manages for the good of the individual. Decision-making can come in many different forms, but it will be oriented toward the idea rather than a hierarchy or a prescribed process.

You might hear someone with a propensity for random system say, *"Creativity and new ideas come from inspiration and exploration."*

Random system intends rapid innovation and prioritizes decisions that are best for the individual. But when overused, random system can become dysfunctional and be experienced as "tyranny of anarchy."

The random system is the one most often and easily judged as "unhelpful." We don't often see it in large organizational systems, and it's therefore the least understood. But small entrepreneurial organizations or research and development teams often function in a high-random system to prioritize creativity and new thinking.

OPERATING SYSTEM SELF-ASSESSMENT

There will often be one or two Operating Systems that we prefer, and one system that we use less — we may even have a bias against it.

Think of a specific team or group of people you interact with on a regular basis. In the context of this group, explore how likely you are to use each of the three Operating Systems. Are you more likely to prioritize rules and processes (closed), collaboration and participation (open), or ideas themselves (random)?

Group context: _____

In this context, what is my operating system usage most likely to look like?

Operating System	Most likely	Slightly Likely	Least Likely
Open System			
Closed System			
Random System			

Personal context: _____

In my personal life, what operating system am I more or less likely to use with a close friend, relative, life partner, or spouse?

Operating System	Most likely	Slightly Likely	Least Likely
Open System			
Closed System			
Random System			

Deepening Insights

Reflect on the two different contexts. What's similar and what's different about your operating system choice in each context?

Which of these operating systems feels more "like you" — i.e., how you would like to operate if there were no other outside forces or expectations on you?

Deepening Insights
OPEN SYSTEM

Use this space to reflect on the following questions:

- What's it like for you when open system is in use?

- What's it like for you when it's missing or underused?

- In what situations do you bring open system?

- In what situations do you dislike open system?

- What do you appreciate about open system?

- What, if any, judgments do you hold about open system and its usefulness?

Deepening Insights
CLOSED SYSTEM

Use this space to reflect on the following questions:

- What's it like for you when closed system is in use?

- What's it like for you when it's missing or underused?

- In what situations do you bring closed system?

- What do you appreciate about closed system?

- What are the beliefs you hold about closed system?

- What, if any, judgments do you hold about closed system?

Deepening Insights
RANDOM SYSTEM

Use this space to reflect on the following questions:

- What's it like for you when random system is in use?

- What's it like for you when it's missing or underused?

- In what situations do you bring random system?

- What do you appreciate about random system?

- What are the beliefs you hold about random system?

- What, if any, judgments do you hold about random system?

Reflection Time

Remember that Structural Dynamics is about the behavioral actions we take in the moment. In order to bring about change in our behavior, it's helpful to be able to see more clearly what we are doing and why we are doing it as we are doing it.

Operating Systems can be changed, but they are pretty core to how we engage with others. They are often strongly influenced by the Operating Systems used in our family life growing up. You may have had parents or caretakers that used highly closed systems with lots of rules, or you may have been given lots of freedom and autonomy to make your own choices. In either case, you might find yourself now appreciating the systems you grew up with and want to replicate them. Or, you might feel frustrated by those systems you grew up with and want to lean away from them at all costs.

Use this space to reflect on the experiences and stories that influence your behavior choices today.

What is your most dominant Operating System? How has this Operating System come to be so strong for you? Reflect on the story that likely sits behind why this system is core for you.

Reflection Time

What was the predominant Operating System in your family growing up?

What impact did it have on you?

Do you see yourself replicating or resisting that Operating System now?

What is the dominant Operating System used in your workplace? What is your evidence for this?

Does the Operating System in your organization match or clash with your own preference? What has your experience of working in this system been?

Level 3:
Communication Domains

We often hear people say, "words matter." And it's true! The words we use convey what matters to us and what's most important to us at the moment. This is the third level of Structural Dynamics: the Communication Domain.

The Communication Domain encompasses the way we name or code the language we are using in a speech act. It is also the greatest source of misunderstanding or miscommunication within our conversations. If you've ever had the experience of being in a conversation with someone and feeling like they were talking past you, it's likely that you were each speaking from a different domain of communication. On the flip side, if you've ever spoken with a group of people and felt like you were all saying the same thing, it's likely that you were all speaking from the same domain.

So, learning to recognize what domain you and others are speaking from at any given moment (and why!) is a pivotal part of developing your communication skills.

There are three domains:

Affect:
Affect is the language of connection and concern for others — feelings and relationships. Its focus and intention is on how others feel about something or how the relationship will be impacted by something.

An example of someone speaking from within the domain of affect might sound like, *"What will the impact of this decision be on the team?"*

Power:
Power is the language of action and completion. The intent is on competency and efficacy and its focus is on getting things done and influencing others.

An example of someone speaking from within the domain of power might sound like, *"What will we do next, by when, and who will be responsible?"*

Meaning:
Meaning is the language of logic and reasoning. The intent and focus are on identity, purpose, and integration.

An example of someone speaking from within the domain of meaning might sound like, *"What's our vision for this project? Why would we take something like this on?"*

COMMUNICATION DOMAINS IN ACTION...

If you asked a CEO why they were getting ready to start an Agile Transformation, here are some responses you might hear, each from a different Communication Domain:

"We're taking on this initiative because...

"I care about our people, and I want to create a better connected and more collaborative work culture for them."	**Affect**
"We need to become more efficient and effective in our work, and we need to reduce the time it takes to launch new features."	**Power**
"I see agility as critical to truly fulfilling our vision and mission as an organization.	**Meaning**

NOTES

COMMUNICATION DOMAINS SELF-ASSESSMENT

Many of us will value all three Communication Domains, but there will likely be an "order" in which we pay attention to them. In other words, in some instances I might value the impact on others over making progress on something. This doesn't mean I don't value getting something done, it just means it's not the first place my thinking goes in every instance.

To explore your relationship to the three Communication Domains, think of a specific team or group of people you interact with on a regular basis in your work setting. In the context of this group, explore how likely you are to speak from each of the three Communication Domains. Are you more likely to prioritize feelings and relationships (affect), action and completion (power), or identity and purpose (meaning)?

Get ready to explore your responses on the following page.

Group context: _____

In this group context, what Communication Domain am I more or less likely to use?

Communication Domain	Most likely	Slightly Likely	Least Likely
Affect			
Power			
Meaning			

Personal context: _____

In this personal context, what Communication Domain am I more or less likely to use with a close friend, relative, life partner, or spouse?

Communication Domain	Most likely	Slightly Likely	Least Likely
Affect			
Power			
Meaning			

Deepening Insights

Reflect on the two different contexts explored above. What's similar and what's different about your language choice in personal and professional spaces and relationships?

Which of these Communication Domains feels more "like you" — i.e., how you would talk if there were no other outside forces or expectations on your communication?

What is your most dominant Communication Domain?

Based on your life experiences, what is your story about how this particular domain has come to be so strong for you? (If you're tempted to skip this section because "you're not sure," just take your best guess! Make up a story about why you might prefer this Communication Domain. You can't get it wrong, and no one will be checking your work!)

What is the dominant Communication Domain used in your workplace?

Does it match your dominant domain, or is it in conflict with it? What has your experience of this dominant workplace domain been? How does it impact the way you communicate with others in your workplace?

The Shadow Side of Communication Domains

Each Communication Domain is helpful and is needed in conversation. But when one or two of them are overused, it's often at the expense of another.

When I work with teams, I often ask them to talk about each of these domains and what it's like when one domain is predominant in a conversation. Below is a summary of some of the most frequently used words and phrases I hear from people as they describe the domains that are not their predominant one.

Read through the table below and make notes next to the words that resonate with you. While you're at it, add additional words you might use to describe each domain.

Someone speaking in...	Intends...	Sounds like...	Words and phrases frequently used to describe the conversation. Someone high in...		
			Affect might say...	Power might say...	Meaning might say...
Affect	Relationship Empathy Care Well-being Love	"How will people feel about this action?"	Feel heard and seen Included Acknowledged	Shallow Mediocre Expendable Lost — not sure how to help Difficult to decipher	It's dangerous to make decisions this way Off topic
Power	Getting things done Productivity Competency Efficacy Completion	"Who's going to make sure this gets done?"	Steamrolled Directive Driven Heartless Intimidating	Accomplished Results Oriented Efficient	Overwhelmed Confused Rushed Overbearing
Meaning	Ideas Integrated thought Thinking Logic Vision Strategy Purpose	"This campaign is the right one because it's aligned to our strategic direction."	Detached Obtuse Analysis Paralysis	All talk, no Action Useless Lofty Unbounded Circular	Aligned Informed Context and purpose are clear Clear

Reflection Time

As you consider your intent and your likely impact on those who speak from a different Communication Domain than you, how have you experienced this playing out in your work relationships? Is there some way that it has tripped you up?

Where might your preference for a certain domain in a specific context have done harm to others?

Level 4: Childhood Stories

In Structural Dynamics, the fourth level of behavior is known as "childhood stories." This is the most invisible part of our behavior, and yet it's always in the room with us — sometimes more so than others.

Build Your Model For Leading Change

For those of you who are thinking, "did I mistakenly pick up a book on psychotherapy?" or are wondering why there is a whole section devoted to talking about childhood in a book about leadership and change, I'll ask you to hang with me for just a few more minutes. Don't skip this section! Let me be clear — this is not therapy. I would assert, instead, that it is about deeply knowing yourself and why you do what you do.

This is about being able to talk about why you do the things you do — without shame, judgment, or blame — so that you do not inadvertently and unknowingly shame, judge, and blame others.

We do what we do for good reasons: because how we grew up taught us specific lessons about how we need to behave in order to survive. As adults, therefore, the same patterns and behaviors we learned as children play out in our conversations with others.

Think for a moment about the worst encounter you've ever had with a leader in your career. Maybe it was your boss or just someone you worked with. Perhaps they were a leader who flew off the handle yelling at a co-worker who was trying to support them. Or a leader who blamed others for everything that was going wrong. Or a leader who abandoned the situation just when they were most needed. We've likely all encountered a leader who left a wake in their path.

But here's the thing: it's easier to see these behaviors in others. If we're really honest, we all have variations of these behaviors in ourselves as well.

For far too long, we have created an artificial barrier between our work and our personal lives. But we cannot talk about growing leadership in ourselves if we are not willing to look at our behavior. Our behavior is what sits at the core of every relationship we have at work and at home. It is the key to being able to engage in conversations that propel us forward or hold us back, and to lead change in a way that is sustainable rather than exhausting and forced.

So, why would you explore and become more aware of your childhood stories?

- So that, as leaders, we do less harm — and know the harm we can do.

- So that we do not create harmful situations for others.

- So that we don't act out our past difficulties on those we interact with and care about today.

- So that we do our own work in order to be able to take responsibility for the impact we have.

Simply put, it would be irresponsible to leave the realm of childhood stories out of any exploration into why we do what we do.

This section is about gaining command of your stories so they don't have command over you.

"The past is never dead. It's not even past."

William Faulkner

A NOTE ON STARTING WHERE YOU ARE — AND MOVING FORWARD GENTLY

In my experience, those starting to explore their childhood stories sit along a long continuum. At one end of the continuum, there will be those of you who have already found your palms a little sweaty and your pulse increased just reading this section. And this may not be the first time you've felt this way while using this workbook.

If this sounds like you, be sure to have support structures in place for yourself as you begin to explore and journal on your childhood stories. This could include your thinking partner — with some designed criteria for how you would like them to listen to and hear you during this process. You may even seek out a trained and certified professional — a coach who is trained in story work — or a therapist, who can support your exploration. Do not go this journey alone!

At the other end of the continuum are those of you who might be thinking, "I don't think I have a childhood story of imperfect love. I'm grateful for my childhood and I feel pretty blessed! I don't think this section is for me."

If this is you, I'll just share this: I found myself having the same thoughts when I was first introduced to this model! So I can identify with what you're feeling. But I'm here to tell you that, while it took me some time to recognize (and I greatly benefited from my own coach acting as a story guide), it turns out that I certainly do have several prominent childhood stories that show up in my behavior today. As a matter of fact, they had been running the show in many ways — especially when I would get into a situation where the pressure was on or the stakes were rising.

Yep, we all have childhood stories. It's just not possible to escape our most formative years without them.

And one more note: to those parents of young children who want to know where in this workbook we will cover "how not to create a childhood story for my kids" — it's just not possible. We are all human, and while we mostly mean well and intend no harm, we are inevitably not perfect.

So, with this context and guidance, begin where you are and when you are ready.

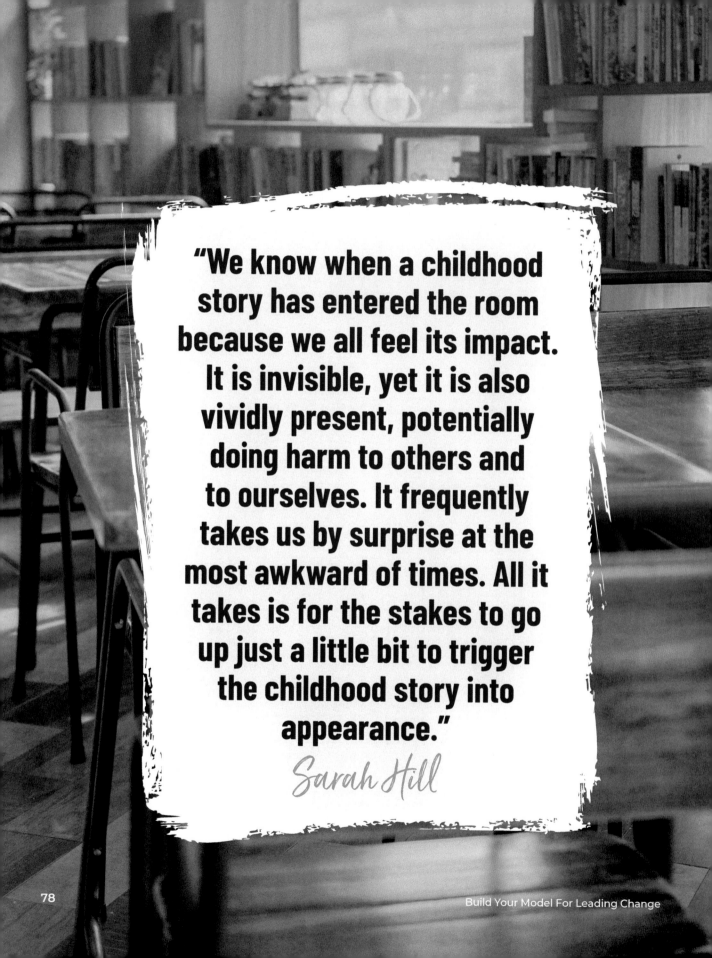

"We know when a childhood story has entered the room because we all feel its impact. It is invisible, yet it is also vividly present, potentially doing harm to others and to ourselves. It frequently takes us by surprise at the most awkward of times. All it takes is for the stakes to go up just a little bit to trigger the childhood story into appearance."

Sarah Hill

THE 3 PARTS OF CHILDHOOD STORIES

Stories are the primary way we make sense of the world. Stories from our childhood (age 0–23) are also where our behavioral preferences are embedded. How we are likely to behave and communicate are patterns laid down early as a direct result of our experiences and the stories we have about them.

Our formative childhood experiences have a structural pattern, one that emerges in our adult life. And when it emerges, it can trigger a childhood story from the past that has a direct impact on how we understand or react to what's happening in the present.

Sarah Hill, in her book *Where Did You Learn to Behave Like That?* (Dialogix, 2017), describes this process beautifully. She says, "We know when a childhood story has entered the room because we all feel its impact. It is invisible, yet it is also vividly present, potentially doing harm to others and to ourselves. It frequently takes us by surprise at the most awkward of times. All it takes is for the stakes to go up just a little bit to trigger the childhood story into appearance."

In her book, Sarah Hill identifies three parts of how childhood stories work: The Immutable Childhood Story, the Old Internal Narrative, and the New Internal Narrative. Each of these facets need to be engaged if we are to understand how our childhood stories are showing up in our behaviors and communication patterns today.

The Immutable Childhood Story is the story of imperfect love. We all have at least one. It can be anything from the smallest disappointment in our childhood to the gravest abuse — and it's the impact of this story that gets triggered when we are under pressure.

The immutable childhood story embodies a child's actual experiences. For example, a child who experienced their parents arguing and eventually witnessed their parents' divorce may have an immutable childhood story about the loss of a family unit.

But the immutable childhood story is rarely just one event. It's often an episodic series of experiences that connect and weave themselves into a thread that, over time, forms into an Old Internal Narrative about ourselves.

For example, the child who experienced the divorce of their parents might have an old internal narrative that says, "Careful who you disagree with! If you make them mad they will ultimately leave you."

Examples of other Old Internal Narratives might include:

- "The only way to succeed is to push others out of the way."

- "To oppose or be opposed is dangerous."

- "I'm only lovable if I'm agreeable."

- "I am not in charge of my own fate."

- "In order to be loved I must be the best."

- "I'm too different to be loved."

- "I'm too bossy to be loved."

- "I must be the peacekeeper if there is to be peace."

As you can see from just these few examples, it's easy for these Old Internal Narratives to have a profound effect on how we behave and engage with others.

But Old Internal Narratives are not insurmountable. The way to gain agency over them is to write a New Internal Narrative. This new narrative helps replace the old narrative so you can gain command in the moment. With a new internal narrative in place, the childhood story no longer has the power to derail and sabotage the current moment.

Examples of New Internal Narratives might include:

- "I create deeper relationships by inviting opposition and disagreement into the room."

- "I am always at choice, even if it doesn't feel like it."

- "I am successful when we are successful."

- "I create peace by inviting truths into the room."

NOTES

Deepening Insights
THE IMMUTABLE CHILDHOOD STORY

My Personal Journey Line

Tell the story of your personal journey, from your earliest memory to early adolescence (~age 23). What were the high points of your young life? What were the low points? Make notes of who the important people were in your life. What were your most memorable times and milestones?

Use the following questions to explore further...

What are you aware of as you look back on your journey line?

What are you most proud of from your childhood?

What were your most difficult times? What made them difficult?

What is something that you experienced as a child that you can identify as shaping your perspective on how you should behave?

NOTES

THE OLD INTERNAL NARRATIVE

What are some possible "Old Internal Narratives" that you hold onto today that served you when you were growing up? Use this space to capture possible narratives as they emerge for you.

Deepening Insights

Use the space below to explore how an Old Internal Narrative you identified in the previous prompt shows up in your life.

- How does it shape the way you behave toward others?

- How does it impact the choices you make in your work life?

- How has it shaped your expectations for how other people should behave toward you?

Story Work Guidance: Story work is ongoing. You may put this section down and come back to it over and over. Moreover, throughout the rest of this workbook, you will periodically be pointed back to your childhood stories. Each time, there is an opportunity to explore a bit deeper.

If you would like to explore the level of childhood story even further, I would encourage you to refer to Sarah Hill's *Where did you Learn to Behave Like That?*

Revisiting the 4 Levels of Behavior

Congratulations! You are now familiar with the four levels of behavior at the core of Structural Dynamics. You have met the four Action Modes, the three Operating Systems, and the three Communication Domains, and you have explored the role that Childhood Stories have in our everyday lives.

While the process of learning to identify and work with these structures of behavior and communication is an ongoing process — life long, even! — you have started an incredibly impactful journey that will take you far when it comes to navigating conversational dynamics. When we can make sense of what's happening in the moment and name what's happening in the moment, we can move forward more productively when we find ourselves stuck.

Build Your Model For Leading Change

NOTES

"Owning our story can be hard but not nearly as difficult as spending our lives running from it."
Brene Brown

CHAPTER 2
Discovering Your Behavioral Model

Build Your Model For Leading Change

BUILDING FUNCTIONAL SELF-AWARENESS

In Chapter 1, you developed awareness around what Action Modes, Operating Systems, and Communication Domains you are likely to use and why, and you delved into how the childhood stories you carry with you inform the ways you are likely to read the room.

Now it's time to build on the assessments and thinking from the last chapter to deepen your awareness about self and others. You will do this by exploring seven critical steps ("junctures") that David Kantor has identified along the road to what he calls "functional self-awareness."

Functional self-awareness is a way of seeing yourself fully, understanding how you relate to others, and taking responsibility for your impact — and it is critical to develop in order to lead and support change.

These junctures are your roadmap for deepening your awareness and form the core of your personal behavioral model.

THE 7 CRITICAL JUNCTURES

You're about to embark on a personal journey to deepen your self-awareness. How long it takes isn't as important as the clarity I hope it brings you. This is about being able to navigate relationships with others, and it's worth every minute you spend on the process.

In **Juncture 1**, you'll be expanding your behavioral repertoire. Where do you notice your behavior? Where does it change? What behaviors come really easily for you? Which ones are you challenged by?

In **Juncture 2**, your task will be to begin to catch sight of the difference between your intent and your impact. What we intend does not always match the behavioral action we take in the room. This juncture is about learning where this disparity shows up for you. Here, you'll explore what's possible when you proactively seek feedback from others rather than being a passive receiver of feedback. It's critical that you be willing to take responsibility for your impact on others.

In **Juncture 3**, you will deep dive into conflict. Conflicts are often simply "model clashes" — where different models are in play for each of the participants. In this section, you will start to become aware of these clashes, identify where you experience them most, and learn to "code" them using the four levels of behavior discussed in Chapter 1.

Clearly, conflicts don't just happen because you dislike something or someone. They happen for good reason. In your life's journey, you will likely have encountered moments that created a narrative for you about yourself and about human dynamics — and as we saw in the last chapter, that narrative can play out in your interactions as an adult. In **Juncture 4**, therefore, you'll explore the possible sources of your childhood stories. What themes existed around these stories and how are they playing out in your relationships today?

Knowing the source of childhood stories helps us make sense of why and when the stakes rise for us in any given moment. In **Juncture 5**, you'll explore your own stakes-raising themes, identify what's different about your behavior in high stakes versus low stakes, and begin to honor and appreciate your "shadow" — and take responsibility for it.

In **Juncture 6**, the work to do is expanding your tolerance for difference. Where do you encounter people with different models from your own? How can you expand your ability to STAY with the difference — even when it shows up as conflict — and work with it, rather than allow it to derail, trigger, or undermine the conversation and relationship?

The final juncture, **Juncture 7**, is about linking your work and personal relationships. What from the work you've done here, in this workbook, will you share with others? How might sharing it be helpful for others to understand you? What are you more curious about in others — especially those you work with — now that you've done this work?

While the graphical representation in this book looks like a set of linear steps, they are anything but linear and certainly not separate. A more accurate way to depict their relationship might be a Venn diagram with a messy spaghetti platter of links to different aspects and concepts within and between the different junctures.

As you reflect and deepen your understanding of each of these junctures, I would invite you to create ways to flip back and forth and reference thinking in one juncture with thinking in another. You'll see myriad opportunities that I've built in for you, but perhaps you'll catch sight of even more. What connections can you make between the junctures?

KANTOR'S 7 CRITICAL
FOR FUNCTIONAL

1
Expanding your behavioral repertoire

3
Recognizing model clashes and their repetitive patterns

2
Recognizing and taking responsibility for your impact on others

JUNCTURES
SELF-AWARENESS

4

Discover your childhood stories and their dominant structures

7

Linking work and personal relationships

5

Know your behavior in high stakes and take responsibility for your shadow

6

Expanding your tolerance for difference

1 Expanding your behavioral repertoire

Back in Chapter 1, when exploring the 4 Levels of Behavior of Structural Dynamics, you took either (or both!) the self-assessment or the bMaps assessment to determine your predominant behavior in Action Modes, Operating Systems, and Communication Domains.

In the first juncture of functional self-awareness, the goal is to build on what you learned in Chapter 1 to actually expand your behavioral range.

Through the work of this juncture, you will feel more prepared to invite a greater range of behaviors and actions into your everyday conversations.

To prepare for the reflections ahead, take a moment to revisit your reflections from Chapter 1.

Go ahead and set some intentions for yourself.

Expanding Your Repertoire:
ACTION MODES

MOVE

- When do you find it easy to put forward ideas?

- In what contexts do you withhold your ideas?

- How often are you the first to speak?

- What's the impact this has on others?

- Do you invite differing points of view?

OPPOSE

- What's it like for you when you disagree with the direction a conversation is going?

- What's it like for you to clearly voice your point of view, even if it's opposing someone else's?

- In what situations is it easier? More difficult?

- Do you see value in voicing push-back on ideas?

FOLLOW

- What's it like for you to voice support or build on the ideas of others?

- What's important for you about voicing support?

- When do you find it more difficult to voice support?

- When do you find it easier to voice support?

BYSTAND

- When do you notice yourself bridging competing ideas that have been shared?

- How easy is this for you?

- Can you think of a time where you were able to place yourself on the periphery of a conversation and observe what was happening in the conversation?

- If so, were you able to name what was happening?

NOTES

MOVE

Expanding your repertoire

- What are the situations, if any, where you overuse Move at the expense of creating space for other ideas?

- What are the situations, if any, where you undersuse the action of Move? What does this cost you?

OPPOSE

Expanding your repertoire

Effective Oppose begins with voicing a Follow and Bystand first (which adds more context to the conversation) before offering a clear Oppose and a Move.

It might sound like this:

- **Move:** I'd like to explore this topic in more depth, I think we might be missing something.

- **Follow:** I agree with you that I think we're missing something and I appreciate you catching that.

- **Bystand:** I'm noticing we only have 30 min left.

- **Oppose:** I don't want to take our time now to do that.

- **Move:** Let's put this as the first agenda item on our next meeting, and we'll make time for it there.

A less effective version of Oppose might sound like this:

- **Move:** I'd like to explore this topic in more depth, I think we might be missing something.

- **Oppose:** I disagree, I don't think that's a good idea.

When the response is just offered as an Oppose — without Follow and Bystand — it's hard for the conversation to move forward.

- What are the situations, if any, where you overuse Oppose?

- What are the situations, if any, where you underuse the action of Oppose?

- Reflect on a situation where you didn't Oppose and it caused you trouble. What happened?

- What's something you are learning about the action of Oppose?

- What's your work to do in bringing more or less Oppose into your conversations?

FOLLOW

Expanding your repertoire

If Follow is higher for you:

- Can you think of a time where you may have supported an idea in the meeting but spoke against the idea outside the meeting to a friend or colleague? In this model, that's called a "covert Oppose" — when you voice one action but intend a different action.

- The value of these actions comes from having access to all of them when they are needed in the conversation and from matching your intention with your action. However, we do things like covert Oppose for a reason. Reflecting back on this example:

  - What led you to voice support in the meeting and hold back what you were really thinking?

- What was the impact of not speaking up?

- What's something that would make it easier for you to voice your thinking in the moment?

If Follow is lower for you:

- What are the situations where you are underusing Follow?

- When you hear the word "Follow," what biases do you have about it? What stories do you make up about its value in a conversation?

BYSTAND
Expanding your repertoire

If Bystand is higher for you...

- Check to make sure you are voicing your perspective in the conversation

- In what situations do you Bystand more often? Why might that be?

- Where might Bystanding be replacing the act of bringing your voice into the conversation more clearly? What would it be like to voice a move or an oppose?

If Bystand is lower for you:

- Look for a conversation where you can place yourself on the periphery. Be mindful of where you might be seeing something, but not voicing what you see. Look to create spaces in the conversation where you can name what you're noticing.

Expanding Your Repertoire:
COMMUNICATION DOMAINS

Exercise: Growing Communicative Competence

The goal of Structural Dynamics is to grow your communicative competence and become multilingual in the use of Communication Domains. Communications Domains are often the source of greatest conflict and misunderstanding in relationships at work and at home. So, here is an exercise to get you started on this journey.

Think of a difficult message that you might need to deliver to a team or an individual. Write the message three separate times, one in each Communication Domain.

Difficult message:

Delivered in the domain of Affect:

Delivered in the domain of Meaning:

Delivered in the domain of Power:

Reflection Time

Reflecting on the exercise above:

What was it like to write the message in each domain? Was there one or two domains that were more difficult for you than the others? If so, this might be the domain that you use less.

Now, craft a fourth message that combines all three Communication Domains. Think about the audience — what is their collective Communication Domain? Consider starting in that domain and then bringing in the others.

We often communicate in the language that we prefer, and our word choices reflect the things we care about most in regard to the topic and the context. But remember, the people you are communicating with may see the world differently and value different things. In your personal journey of increasing tolerance for difference, reflect on the following:

- For the Communication Domain that is your least used, who do you know that uses this domain well?

- How might they be able to support you in increasing your use of this domain when needed?

- What are some ways that you can bring more of your least-used Communication Domain into your conversational repertoire?

- What might change in the outcome you get or how the message is received based on which Communication Domain(s) you use?

Expanding Your Repertoire
OPERATING SYSTEMS

What is your preferred operating system (open, closed, random)?
How did your preference for this system come to be?

What's your story behind your preference? Is it similar or different to the system you grew up in?

Reflect on what it would be like to work in a team with the predominant Operating System of OPEN:

What would it be like working in this team?

What would this team do really well?

What would be challenging about working in this team?

Where might open system get in the way?

RANDOM:

What would it be like working in this team?

What would this team do really well?

What would be challenging about working in this team?

Where might random system get in the way?

CLOSED:

What would it be like working in this team?

What would this team do really well?

What would be challenging about working in this team?

Where might closed system get in the way?

Using your reflections about the team Operating Systems you explored above, consider what it would be like to facilitate a meeting for each of these different teams.

- What would each of these teams require of you as the facilitator?

- What would be the greatest challenge for you, personally?

- How would you account for these challenges in your design?

- What strategies would you employ in the situation(s) you find most challenging?

NOTES

2 Recognizing and taking responsibility for your impact on others

Have you ever received feedback from someone and immediately responded with, "But that's not what I meant!"

Trust me, you are not alone.

I believe that none of us will ever build enough self-awareness to rise above, or eliminate, the accidental "ouch that hurt" impact on someone else. But what we can do is get better at suspending our impulse to defend our intent and take full responsibility for the impact. So, rather than defending our intent with "but that's not what I meant" or "if you felt left out from what I did, I'm sorry," we can respond with something like, "I'm sorry my actions caused you to feel left out. I see that."

The first step here is to separate your intent from your impact. They are two different things.

Intent is about who you are. It comes from your motivation, purpose, values, or morals. Your intent will be how you're feeling or what you're thinking at the moment.

Impact is how your actions make someone else feel. The same action can and will be received differently by each person. This is because we receive communication through our individual behavioral model, which includes our own stories about why we do what we do and the stories we make up about why others do what they do.

So, intent is your motivation and what you thought you wanted to do, impact will be the experience or emotion of the other person.

Take responsibility for your intention AND your impact — not just your intention.

It is everyone's responsibility to own both our intent and our impact. But, like many concepts, this is much easier to say and much harder to do.

If you've ever received feedback from someone that the impact of your actions was different than you anticipated, chances are you've thought — and maybe even said — "...but that was not my intention!"

As you've probably noticed in these moments, the feedback we receive about our impact can hit really hard. It can feel like a crisis of identity. If, for example, I see myself as someone who is caring and inclusive but I hear that I've had an impact that feels dismissive or condescending, the feedback will create dissonance.

The way forward is to see such feedback as being about your behavior — not about who you are as a person.

With this understanding, you can take a different action, even if it's just a small one. And by taking a different action, you can make a huge difference in the impact you have and the results you get.

This second juncture plays an important role for us, both individually and collectively. Without developing our ability to own our part in a dynamic, it's impossible to bring about change. We can't just point to other people as the ones who need to change. There will also be something in what we are doing that is contributing to the results we are getting.

> **Here is what it sounds like to NOT take responsibility when offered feedback...**
>
> **Person A:** When you sent that email to the team, it was dismissive and condescending. I felt like you overstepped your role and our boundaries.
>
> **Person B:** But that was not my intent! We had to get the work done, and I was worried about missing our deadline. I just wanted to help and move things along efficiently.

In this situation, Person A is probably walking away from the interaction still upset. They are likely feeling dismissed and unheard.

Person B is likely feeling wrongly accused, like they've been made to be the villain despite their good intentions.

This common breakdown in communication is not just about intent vs. impact. It's also a "model clash" between Person A (who is speaking in the Communication Domain of "affect") and Person B (who is speaking in the Communication Domain of "power").

Here is what it sounds like to TAKE responsibility when offered feedback...

Person A: When you sent that email to the team, it was dismissive and condescending. I felt like you overstepped your role and our boundaries.

Person B. Oh wow, I'm so sorry my email had that impact on you. That certainly was not my intent, but I value your feedback. Thank you for telling me this. Can you tell me more? What was it I said in the email that landed as dismissive and condescending?

Person A: I was already working on getting the task done. Instead of asking me, the person who is responsible for the work, about its status, you just sent the email. You just assumed that the work was not started and asserted that it needs to be done quickly. I feel like there were a lot of unstated assumptions behind your actions, and that they could have been cleared up by simply asking me what the status was.

Person B: I see why it felt like I stepped on you when I jumped to conclusions and took action without first asking about the status of the project. I want to really apologize for having that impact. I'm going to do better at reminding myself to ask instead of assuming in the future.

Person A: Thank you for saying that, I really appreciate it.

In this version of the situation, Person B changes their response and asks an important question: "What did I say that landed for you as dismissive and condescending?" Then, Person B listened and acknowledged that they could see how their email could have the impact that it did — and they apologized for it.

In this conversation, the focus became about Person B learning and understanding their impact, and it was not really focused on their intent at all.

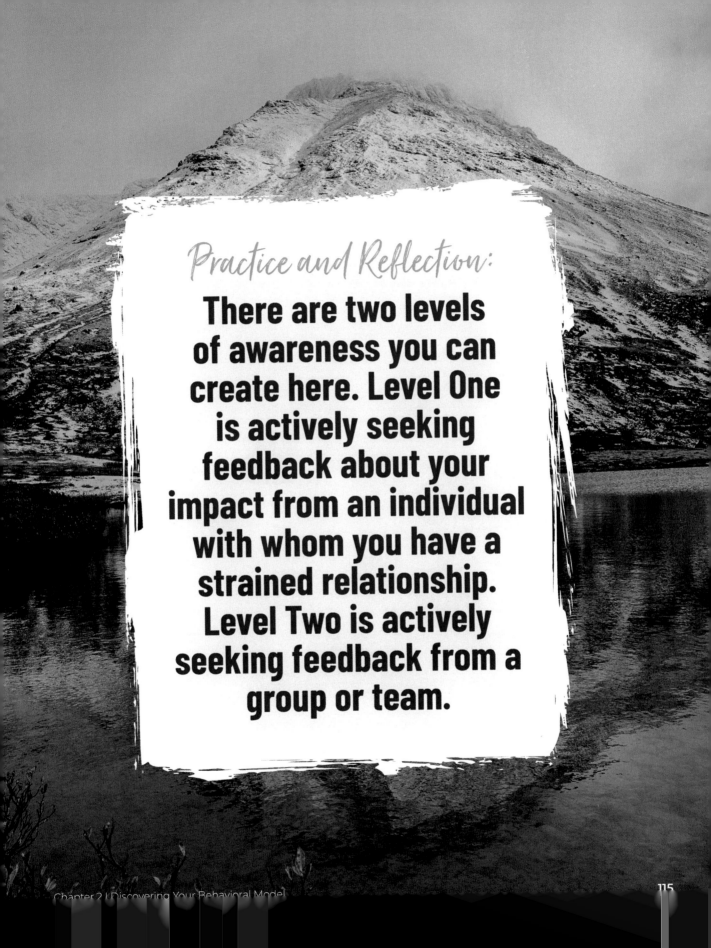

Practice and Reflection:

There are two levels of awareness you can create here. Level One is actively seeking feedback about your impact from an individual with whom you have a strained relationship. Level Two is actively seeking feedback from a group or team.

Level 1 – Individual Relationship

Identify 2–3 individuals with whom you have a relationship that is challenging to you in some way. Maybe it's someone you keep having the same conversation with, or you notice that every time you leave a conversation with them it has had a negative impact on you.

Seek feedback from them by asking, "What is it I do that makes you behave toward me the way that you do?"

David Kantor calls this circular causal inquiry. Think of it like Newton's third law: "every action has an equal and opposite reaction." Every behavior we get that we don't like — well, we are also playing a part in creating it.

The goal is to discover any hurtful or harmful impact you may have. This action also signals your willingness to take responsibility for your part.

Identify the 2–3 individuals here.

Reflection Time

Reflect on what you hear in your feedback conversations with the individuals you identified above. Capture your learning and insights here.

Level 2 – Team Relationship

We show up differently in one-on-one relationships than we do in teams. If you are in a position to lead a team meeting or facilitate a team conversation, then select a team that you enjoy working with and select a team that you find more challenging in some way.

At the end of a meeting, ask for impact feedback from the group. You might say something like, "I'm working on gaining a greater awareness of my behavior in team meetings and I would like your feedback."

Then ask them to give you some feedback in this format:

When you did,   <behavior, action>

the impact on me was   <emotion, feeling>

We share this model with facilitators who lead meetings and ask them to carve out opportunities in their work to pause and ask for some brief impact feedback at the end of a meeting. Your response in receiving impact feedback should be, "Thank you for sharing that." Refrain from justifying or defending what you did in that moment (as hard as that might be).

Reflection Time

Reflect on what you hear from these conversations and capture your learning or insight.

3 Recognizing model clashes and their repetitive patterns

Have you ever been in a conversation with someone where it feels like you're stuck having the same conversation over and over again?

Or have you experienced conversations that — despite everybody's best intentions — result in misunderstandings or create confusion and uncertainty? If so, then chances are you have stumbled into what David Kantor calls "model clash."

Model clash happens when there is a difference between one behavioral model and another behavioral model. In some instances, we can tolerate the difference. But in other cases, often as the stakes begin to rise for us, the difference can turn into model clash. For example, when someone speaking from the Communication Domain of "power" is engaging with someone who is speaking from the domain of "meaning," or when one person is using a "random" operating system and the other is working from a "closed" operating system.

When it comes to model clash in the realm of our behavioral models, the Communication Domains and Operating Systems are ripe places for differences to emerge between two or more people — after all, these are the realms where we signal what matters to us and where we might discover that we hold different ideas about how people should or should not work together!

Whenever we're engaging with someone who is speaking from a different behavioral model than we are, we are at risk for model clash. In other words: conflict.

And this is why Structural Dynamics is so helpful. It gives us a lens to see and decode what's happening in the moment so that we can better understand our repetitive patterns and the stories behind them. With this understanding comes the ability to adjust, make considered choices, and get better results from our conversations.

Identifying model clashes and their repetitive patterns

Think about a recent conversation where you felt misunderstood, where you and the other participant(s) were talking past each other, or where you experienced conflict. Now, consider the following questions:

What about this conversation felt frustrating to you?

What emotions were you feeling in the moment as the conflict emerged?

Have you noticed that you have this kind of conversation repeatedly with the individual or group you were speaking to?

A MODEL CLASH IN ACTION

Below, listen to what it might sound like when there is a model clash between Operating Systems.

The Conversation:

Tom: I just need people to stop complaining about things like the color of the break room walls and get on with their work. If I have to respond to one more email about some insignificant issue in this building, I'm going to lose it. Why do we always need to seek input on everything we do? It's very inefficient.

Jada: You keep getting those emails because you're not listening to people. People voice concerns, but they never get any closure about what's being done about the issue. Instead, they get yelled at for bringing the issue up! This response just further drives their disgruntlement.

Tom: I listen and I take action, Jada. But no one ever acknowledges any of the work that happens to make their lives better here at work.

Jada: You're missing the point. This isn't about you. It's about the employees not feeling heard. Have you ever considered that just acknowledging the issue that's bothering them would be helpful?

JR: I agree with Jada on this. At least once a week, I'm having a conversation with someone who feels like their suggestions are just being ignored. They would be okay if they are not done, they just want to know that someone is listening. They want to know if the suggestion is being considered and, if so, when a decision might be made.

The Players:

Tom: Tom just wants someone to establish the parameters so he can be more efficient. He is operating from a "closed" system.

Jada: Jada wants to prioritize having people's voices heard. She is operating from an "open" system.

JR: JR is also speaking from an "open" operating system and takes the Action Mode of "follow" in this scenario to build on Jada's assessment of the situation.

VOCAL SIGNATURES AND CODING CONVERSATIONS

In Chapter 1, we broke apart the levels of behavior and structures of communication in order to understand them each on their own terms. But as the model clash example between Tom, Jada, and JR shows, all the levels of behavior and communication show up in conversation — often in the span of a single sentence or two!

So what's most helpful when it comes to recognizing model clash is to start putting the levels of behavior and structures of communication together and developing your capacity to code behavior in the moment.

Action Modes / Operating Systems / Communication Domains

Every sentence we speak can be coded with some combination of these first three levels of behavior. We'll add in "childhood stories" when we move to Juncture 4. But for now, watch how "real-time" coding can happen:

"Let's move on to the next topic."	"I disagree with this direction. I need to understand the purpose better so that I can decide if it makes sense for me to participate."	"I can support that, and I think others will feel supportive as well if we ask them what they think."
Action Mode: **Move** — because it's setting a direction **Operating System:** **Closed** — because it's not asking for any input **Communication Domain:** **Power** — because it's about action **Putting the levels together: Move** in Closed Power	**Action Mode:** **Oppose** — because it's disagreeing with the direction **Operating System:** **Random** — because it's based on what's needed for the individual **Communication Domain:** **Meaning** — because it's seeking context and purpose **Putting the levels together: Oppose** in Random Meaning	**Action Mode:** **Follow** — because it's getting behind (offering support for) the previous idea **Operating System:** **Open** — because it's focus is on asking for input from others **Communication Domain:** **Affect** — because it's concerned with how people will feel as a result of the action **Putting the levels together:** **Follow** in Open Affect

When we're able to describe our behavior — and others' behavior — in these terms, it comes to life in a really simple way. It allows us to see where our communication patterns are propelling us forward and where we might be getting stuck in the overuse of one or more levels.

This is where vocal signatures come in.

Our vocal signature consists of our prefered Operating System and Communication Domain. Knowing our vocal signature gives us a leg up in being able to skillfully navigate model clashes.

The following table is designed to help you find your vocal signature. By doing so, you will be well on your way to learning how to hear and bridge to someone else when they are speaking from a different vocal signature.

	Open	Closed	Random
Affect	Freely express emotions; all emotions are important; it's important everyone describes their feelings.	Emotions are appropriate in the right place and intensity; no need to repeat expressed emotions; consistency in emotional expression; self-control.	Feelings are in the moment; intimacy is right when it's right; fun and hilarity; emotions can help drive the creative process.
Power	Getting things done through others; teams are the functional unit; decisions are best by consensus.	Clear direction and goals are to be followed; hierarchy illustrates the distribution of influence; chain of command; command and control; measurements of performance to provide feedback.	Do what works for the situation; consistency blocks innovation; do your own thing; agreements are often not kept due to loss of interest; tangents are good and can inform; working as a team slows individuals down; lack of predictability in methods; empowerment.
Meaning	Values oriented toward inclusion, including: democracy; community; people as the most important asset; focusing on the process to reap rewards; Bill of Rights; services; responsiveness to market; caring.	Values oriented toward competence, including: results; effectiveness and efficiency; personal accountability; respect; tradition; vision; clear roles and responsibilities; continuous quality improvement; professionalism; no loose ends; coherence and consistency.	Values oriented toward individual creativity, including: innovation; freedom; cutting-edge thinking; do the right thing. Can be perceived as "philosophy du jour."

EXERCISE

Coding your conversation

Are you ready to try coding a conversation?

Reflect on a conversation you've had that didn't go well — where it seemed like you and the other person were talking past one another.

In the left-hand column below, write down what was said in the moment by you and by the other person(s) in the conversation. In the right-hand column, try to identify what Action Mode, Operating System, and Communication Domain was being used in the moment.

What was said:	How you would code it? Action Mode: Move, Follow, Oppose, Bystand Operating System: Closed, Open, Random Communication Domain: Power, Affect, Meaning

EXERCISE

What was the model clash you might have been experiencing?

Model clashes that raise the stakes for us in a situation often do so when we start to judge the behaviors of the other person or assert that our point of view is the only "right" way to look at the situation. This is where our intolerance for difference shows up (a process we'll explore in detail in Juncture 6). For now, reflect on the situation you explored above. In what ways were you judging the actions or behaviors of the other person?

Engaging in a cross-model conversation

The goal of Juncture 3 is to learn to identify model clashes as they are happening so that you can learn to engage in effective "cross-model conversations."

David Kantor defined cross-model conversations as a very specific way of engaging in dialogue. It is grounded in the idea that differences between how two people view something are not a problem if the people have a way to navigate them. As a matter of fact, difference is needed if we're to build communicative competence and access the collective intelligence that exists in any given group.

We can begin a cross-model conversation simply by bridging to the Communication Domain and/or Operating System that the other person is using.

Bridging is especially useful when the other person is speaking from a Communication Domain or Operating System that is not our dominant one. For example, if I know I'm getting ready to talk to my boss, who often speaks in Closed Power (concise, efficient, and action oriented), I'm likely not going to be very successful starting my conversation from the language of Open Affect (wanting to acknowledge everyone's feelings).

Imagine if I said, "With the possibility of the upcoming re-org in the next few weeks, I'm worried about our managers. Let's get everyone together to talk about strategies for supporting our staff." My boss, working in Closed Power, might simply stop listening at the phrase, "let's get everyone together." But what if, instead, I started with something like this: "In light of the upcoming re-org, our managers are going to need some clear support strategies to help them know where to direct people when they have questions. I think it might be a more efficient use of everyone's time and better set them up for success if we had a brief meeting to talk through some of those strategies." In this second example, I'm shifting my language to be more about efficiency, but I'm still bringing in my move about gathering in an open system. This is my bridge — I've made my move in the language of the other person so that it can be heard and explored more effectively.

Bridging to a different Communication Domain and Operating System is one way to get started in a cross-model conversation. **But there's another core component of holding effective conversations: being able to inquire into the other person's perspective**. This means learning to shift from defending our point of view to suspending our point of view and being curious about the other person's point of view. In other words, developing the skill of shifting from "advocacy" to "inquiry."

FROM ADVOCACY Which looks like...	TO INQUIRY Which looks like...
Being right	Learning
Move / Oppose	Bystand / Follow
Being "politically" motivated	Entering a state of curiosity
Blaming	Taking responsibility
Thinking, "Here is how you must change..."	Asking, "How can I change?"
Assuming there is only one "best idea" ... and it's mine	Entertaining multiple and contradictory ideas simultaneously
Defending against my own shadows and stories	Acknowledging the existence of my shadows and stories
Fragmentation	Wholeness

Being able to hold a cross-model conversation can be a challenge. When we are at our best and most self-aware, we can hear someone speaking from an "open" Operating System and bridge to that system — meaning, for example, that we can speak from their open system and then bring in our closed system perspective. In these moments, we are able to skillfully engage across differing behavioral models and hold an effective cross-model conversation.

On our worst days, however, or when the stakes are high for us on an individual level, we might struggle to have an effective cross-model conversation. We may not be as fluid in our communicative competence. We might feel triggered and fall into our high-stakes behavioral model, which we'll talk more about in Juncture 5.

Notably, cross-model conversations are not just about open conflict and hostility. Sometimes it's as simple as when you feel like you're talking past each other instead of talking with each other — where you may be aligned on the objective, but using words that the other person is not able to hear.

We often speak in the structural language that we prefer and that makes the most sense to us, whether it is a conscious or an unconscious choice. When we encounter someone with a different model — someone speaking from a different structure — the impact is often that they don't hear us as well as if we were speaking from the same space as them.

CROSS-MODEL CONVERSATION PRINCIPLES

Difference is a key source of learning about ourselves and others.

It is pointless to assert that one model is "better" than another. Every model has its limits, which we must face in order to grow.

The only "bad" model is the one that does not recognize its own limits, wrongly assumes it is complete and does not have to grow, and presumes to be better than other models.

Deepening Insights
CHANGING THE OUTCOME —
CROSS-MODEL CONVERSATIONS

Let's now return to the conversation you wrote out in the exercise at the very beginning of Juncture 3, focusing especially on the Communication Domains that you and the other person(s) were each speaking in.

Now, take a step back and consider the conversation with fresh eyes. When we are speaking in different Communication Domains or Operating Systems, it can feel like the other person just "does not get it" or simply can't see what we see.

Let's see if you can imagine a better outcome. Ready?

Step 1: If you could "re-do" the conversation you identified above, how might you start by bridging to the Communication Domain or Operating System of the other person? What would that sound like?

Step 2: Imagine bringing in additional points from your primary Communication Domain or Operating System. What might this sound like? How might you do this?

Step 3: What are some other ways you could bring in more inquiry? What assumptions might you be making in this conversation? What would be helpful to know about their point of view?

4 Discover your childhood stories and their dominant structures

In your life's journey, you will likely have lived through many experiences that form your immutable childhood stories — these don't change, they are the experiences we lived. And these stories contribute to the creation of our internal narratives — the stories we tell ourselves about who we are, about human behavior, and about how we should interact. As we explored in Chapter 1, these narratives are often laid down in early life (age 0–23).

These narratives play out for us all as adults in the conversations we have, the relationship dynamics we participate in, and the way we see the world — whether we're aware of it or not!

Building on the exploratory work you already did in Chapter 1 to identify one of your childhood stories and the impact it has on your everyday interactions, Juncture 4 is about deepening your understanding of the Old Internal Narratives you have created and identifying the structures behind the childhood stories. This will enable you to see more clearly how they play out in your relationships today.

Why childhood stories matter in the workplace...

In all of his work around communication and relationships, David Kantor, the author of Structural Dynamics, summed up the "childhood stories" level of behavior by posing the questions that sit at the root of all of our conversations and relationships — in work, life, and home:

- Was I loved?

- Am I loved?

- Do I know how to love?

- Do I know how to be loved?

You might be asking, "Do I really need to be loved at work? I mean, come on!"

Well, yes. We all have a fundamental core need to love and be loved. We just don't talk about love in the workplace very often. Of course, depending on the culture and company you work in, you may find that this kind of conversation is not welcomed at all. That's a topic for a different book!

Notably, I'm not advocating for you to walk into work tomorrow and ask your teams if they love you. But I guarantee that your behavior each day poses this very question to your coworkers in any number of different ways.

Let's say I am leading a large change effort and I ask a team to do something that they disagree with, and then three people get really mad at me and won't make eye contact with me as they leave the room. In one scenario, I follow up with them right after the meeting and schedule a 1:1 to ask them why they are mad. In another scenario, I might go tell their boss that they were being really

insubordinate in the meeting and that I need for them to play nice and get along next time, even if they disagree with me. In yet another scenario, I might choose to simply not hold a group meeting the next time I have bad news to deliver — I'll just send an email so I don't have to face their anger.

We might not be using the words "love" in these scenarios — we might not even like the other people we work with. But the behaviors we react with in response to the group's "perceived" anger (after all, we don't really know why they were not making eye contact) is all about wanting to be liked (or loved) — or, at least, avoiding the feeling that we are not liked (or loved). This means that we need to understand our childhood stories and what they're telling us about our behavior choice in a moment when we are triggered.

Our workplace behaviors, in high stakes, will almost invariably be linked to a childhood story of imperfect love. For example, a child who experienced harsh criticism or being made fun of by others may have an Old Internal Narrative that "to be different is lonely." The "structural story" of this childhood story will be one in which she made a Move, only to have her friends "Oppose in Closed Affect" — meaning that they closed off their affect toward her and gossiped about her to one another. Today, as a leader in the room, if she makes a Move to introduce a new change and others in the room respond with outward signs of what she assumes is "displeasure," it may trigger her childhood story. She will likely experience being "opposed in closed affect," just like in her childhood story. This structural similarity may trigger her Old Internal Narrative that "to see things differently is lonely." It will invariably raise the stakes for her.

As a result, her shadow side will emerge: the shadow side of her "high-stakes heroic mode."

Every story has a hero — Heroic modes and their shadows

What's a story without a hero to save the day?

During adolescence and young adult years, as we relive and re-experience our childhood story in many different ways, we will subconsciously be searching for our Heroic Mode — the hero within us who will show up to intervene on behalf of the child. This is the hero who will right the wrongs at the center of the childhood story we keep experiencing.

These Heroic Modes have positive intentions — they have been developed to protect us from the negative impact of our experience. But they also have shadows — light, gray, and dark. When we encounter a high-stakes situation that triggers the childhood story, we will take on characteristics of one (or two) of the Heroic Modes. In the light zone, your heroic identity assumes its most ascendant qualities. It makes you feel vital, authentic, and alive. But as the stakes rise and our behavior slips into the gray zone, the heroic identity becomes tainted — it starts to exhibit both its positive and negative traits. In the dark zone, we are in our "shadow" — the source of all of our biases, doubts, and deepest fears.

The Fixer

The Fixer jumps in to overcome adversity with energy and a willingness to lead from the front. The voice of the fixer says, "I will overcome by sheer will, if necessary."

As the Fixer moves into the gray zone, they move to conqueror. There is a thirst for battle — they insist that their view is "right" and that everyone else should get on board. In the dark zone, or "shadow," the abuser comes forward — they are driven to overcome at whatever the cost, including abuse, rage, violence, corruption through power, and carrying the fight to the enemy.

David Kantor identified three Heroic Modes:

- The Fixer who Overcomes
- The Survivor who Endures
- The Protector who Shields

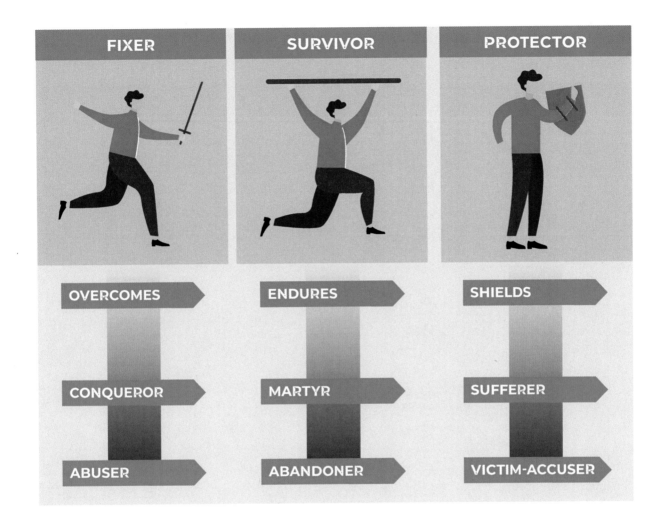

The Survivor

The Survivor's gift is endurance, staying power, and perseverance. The Survivor may believe that nothing holds power over them. The voice of the Survivor says, "I can endure, at the pain of death if necessary."

As the Survivor moves into the gray zone, they become the Martyr: self-sacrificing and willful about their beliefs. In the dark zone, or "shadow," the hero who would endure and persevere now becomes the abandoner — they leave the situation with self-righteousness, abandoning it emotionally, physically, or both.

The Protector

The Protector's gift is shielding, dedication to caring, and being sensitive to the abuse of power. The voice of the Protector says, "I will not stand by idly pretending that our suffering doesn't exist."

As the Protector moves into the gray zone, they become the sufferer or victim, and they petition others for help. In the dark zone, or "shadow," the hero becomes the maudlin victim with a relentless cry for revenge.

CHOOSING YOUR HERO

The Heroic Modes are closely related to the Communication Domains. The Fixer is high in the domain of Power. The Survivor is high in the domain of Meaning, and the Protector is high in the domain of Affect.

If you were really sick, what might you say or do?

"I will carry on as usual" (**Survivor**)

"I will be in bed" (**Protector**)

"I will overcome this illness" (**Fixer**)

Make notes of any judgments you may have about any of the Heroic Modes.

Fill out the matrix below, making notes in each box. It's possible that you may blend two of the Heroic Modes, or you may find that you embody just one of them.

	The Fixer "I WILL"	The Survivor "I CAN"	The Protector "I CAN'T"
Communication Domain	Power	Meaning	Affect
Most Like Me			
Not Quite Like Me			
Definitely Not Me			

ENGAGING THE STRUCTURAL STORY

Now that you have become familiar with the Heroic Modes, we will move into a few key exercises designed for you to start noticing when childhood stories are showing up based on the behavioral structures that give them shape and meaning. As a result, you will start to become more adept at navigating them in a way that will bring you better outcomes in your relationships and conversations.

In Chapter 1, you began the work of identifying an Old Internal Narrative that you carry with you from your childhood — the lesson you have internalized as the result of a childhood experience. Here, you are going to explore the patterns and structures that may sit in the childhood story so that you can more easily locate "triggers" to your "high-stakes behavior" (the topic of Juncture 5).

Every childhood story has a structure.

One of the best ways to gain a deeper awareness of your own childhood stories and behavioral patterns is to tell their structural story. The structural story is the version of the story that you can tell by using the 4 Levels of Behavior. When we're able to tell the structural version, it's easier to see when we're entering potentially triggering territory because of our childhood stories — in other words, when the same structures that sit under our childhood stories have entered the room, even if the context is so radically different that we might not have noticed the parallels.

Guidance on Further Childhood Story Work

This is a gentle reminder. While I'm introducing you to the concept of childhood stories and inviting you to explore yours as a means to experience the confidence, clarity, and freedom that comes from being in command of your own behavior and your ability to lead change, there are a few things to keep in mind:

This is a lifelong, continuous exploration. You will not "complete" it through a few reflection questions in a workbook. Rather, my hope is that you become more curious and open to exploration and finding the linkages between "then" and "now."

There is a whole field of trained and certified professionals — therapists and coaches — who are great guides for diving into questions about our childhood stories and our relationship to love. They will go far deeper than you'll go in this workbook.

Create a support structure for yourself — who will you connect with and talk to if you need support?

Refer to *Where did you Learn to Behave Like That?* by Sarah Hill for more guidance and stories.

When you're ready, deeply exploring your childhood stories is not only a worthwhile journey, it will greatly enhance your ability to lead change. When you react from an old, unexamined internal narrative, you are not in a place to thoughtfully and insightfully carry on a skilled conversation that will yield better results in the future.

Every story has a structure

First, take a moment to revisit the childhood story that you identified in Chapter 1. Go ahead and bring that story forward into this space and reflect on what was happening in the way that you and another person(s) were interacting.

Using the skill of coding conversational structures that you began to hone in Juncture 3, try the same thing here.

In the spaces below, code what was happening in the story according to Action Mode, Operating System, and Communication Domain.

Action Modes: Move, Follow, Oppose, Bystand
- What were the Action Modes you were using in the moment?
- What were the Action Modes being used by the other person(s)?

Every story has a structure

Operating Systems: Open, Closed, Random
- What Operating Systems were in play?
- What was the experience this created for you?
- What did it feel like?

Communication Domains: Power, Affect, Meaning
- What was the Communication Domain you were speaking in?
- What was the Communication Domain being used by the other person(s)?
- What was it like for you?

Deepening Insights

What do you understand differently/better from being able to see the structure of your childhood story?

- Where do you encounter similar structures in your life today?

- How does this structural story show up in your leadership? Do you avoid replicating it at all costs? Do you tend toward it because you see value in it?

- Where does it raise the stakes for you or cause you difficulty in your close relationships?

- How does being able to see the structural story affect your ability to have greater awareness of your behaviors?

Reflection Time

In this juncture, you've spent a considerable amount of time and energy identifying one of your childhood stories and how it shows up for you in your adult life.

Using the space below, consider whether you can see any themes emerging in this story and your other childhood stories — for example, around anger, betrayal, despair, or shame.

- How do these themes show up for you in everyday life?

- Have you been helped or hindered by how these themes show up in your behaviors at work?

- How can they help you identify moments where you are likely to feel triggered?

Structural Story:
The long legacy of the "leave out" game

I had two best friends in elementary school, but one of them would play the "leave out game" every day. This meant that, every day, she would pick one of the two of us to play with while the other one was left to play on our own.

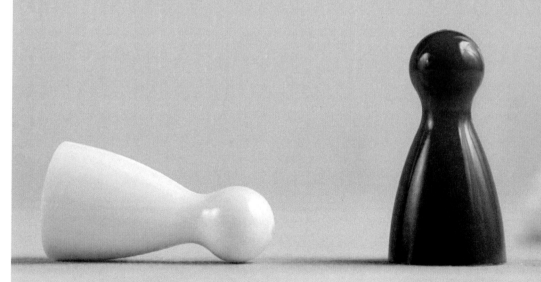

I've always remembered this story, but, as an adult, I never really paid much attention to it. At least, not until I started to do the kind of deeper self-work described in this workbook. Now, as a result of my self-work, I have a much different and better understanding of the role this childhood story has played in my life.

Here's the structure of that childhood story: each day, the one friend would "Move in Closed Power" — meaning, she would make the decision about who got to play together for the day. Meanwhile, I would withdraw and become a silent bystander, a place from which I developed the Old Internal Narrative that "other people get to decide."

Now, in the room as an adult, I can find myself in "high-stakes mode" almost any time I encounter someone who is strong in the Move-Closed-Power structure.

Here's what this looks like: at my first full-time job after college, I was told that I would need 15–20 years of experience before I would qualify for a leadership position. I thought this was ridiculous. It felt like someone was making a unilateral decision about me and my life. It threw me into "high-stakes" mode, and I quit the job.

What was happening for me is that I was reacting to the structure of Move-Closed-Power. The company was telling me its policy. It was a closed system, and the way to get to leadership within this closed system was being clearly defined for me — "work here for 15 more years before we will consider you for this position." Of course, now I can see that the structure of Move-Closed-Power was a trigger for my old narrative that "other people get to decide." As a result, I took on the shadow side of my Heroic Mode: I became the shadow of the

"Survivor." And in high stakes, this shadow makes me feel like I have no other choice but to abandon the situation and take back my control. In a very self-righteous, "I'll show you" kind of way, I asserted my choice-making ability in the best way I could think of: I quit.

And, as luck would have it, I was offered a job in a leadership position for another company.

This became my heroic story, over and over. I created a new internal narrative of "I have a voice," and "I decided." When I would encounter closed power, I would abandon the situation and carve out a new path. It wasn't wrong, and it's certainly a way I've made some good choices in my life. But when it comes to being in longer relationships with others, the idea of abandoning ship doesn't work. I had to learn to "stay in the conversation" — to find my voice within the situation in order to share my perspective and push back on ideas. I needed to find a way to balance my empowering new internal narrative with a greater awareness of the fact that "high stakes" could trigger my shadow into emerging. Without finding this balance, I wasn't actually "making decisions," I was being run by my shadow.

Today, thanks to my self-awareness work about my childhood stories and what creates "high stakes" for me, I can much more easily catch sight of the childhood story I have — the one that says, "other people get to decide." Now, instead of being controlled by my shadow and my impulse to abandon situations where that structure of Move-Closed-Power occurs, I am able to stay in the conversation and offer my perspective through the lens of cross-model conversations. Now, even in high stakes, I exercise far more choice in my behavior and achieve better outcomes as a result.

5 Know your behavior in high stakes and take responsibility for your shadow

Knowing the source of our childhood stories helps us make sense of what creates "high stakes" for us in certain situations. In other words, it helps explain how we get triggered by certain things people say or behaviors they bring into the room.

As Juncture 3 on "model clash" emphasized, Communication Domains and Operating Systems are ripe places for there to be differences between two or more people. This is because Communication Domains are about the words we use that signal what we value, and Operating Systems are about the implicit rules — or norms — that govern how we work together with others. Often, we will have a strong preference for one or two domains and systems, and we will have a negative bias against at least one.

Notably, the negative bias is often laid down in childhood or in early adolescence (a topic you just addressed in detail in Juncture 4) — and it is here that you will find a significant source of high stakes when you're in the room.

When others speak or behave from a Communication Domain or Operating System you have a bias against (i.e., a childhood story about), it can trigger an enormous response. This is because the structure of what's playing out in the here-and-now maps onto a similar structure from a different — typically childhood — context. In these moments, you will be transported to when your younger self had an experience that didn't turn out so well, and you will react with the expectation that you'll have the same results this time.

Low stakes vs. High stakes

Low-stakes conversations are those that feel "easier." We feel more relaxed and in command of our behavior. Perhaps it's because we don't have a high personal investment in the outcome, or because we are in conversation with a person or group with a high degree of interpersonal trust and a track record for hearing out everyone's perspectives.

"High stakes," by contrast, are those times when we are drawn, almost involuntarily, into a space of high anxiety, vigilance, upset, and reactivity. At the extreme end of high stakes, the response is physical — elevated pulse and sweaty palms — and it feels like your very survival is at stake. In medium stakes, it might be more like a conflict of dominance based on the rules of order (or the language of rules) we are using. And in low stakes, we might see differences between perspectives, but the conflict feels like it's simply a matter of compatibility rather than dominance or survival.

Factors that raise the stakes

The stakes can rise for us in three primary areas:

- **Events that happen in our exterior context (environmental or organizational).**

Our environmental context includes things like natural disasters, political battles, shifts in economy, big changes in the market, etc. Organizational context includes things like changes in your job or company, re-organizations, corporate downsizing, etc.

- **Events that happen in interpersonal dynamics between individuals.**

Factors here can include holding tightly to a desired outcome, challenges to our preferred Operating System, and differences in the Communication Domain that move us from "model difference" to "model clash" ("model clash" being where we find the moral judgment about the difference we are experiencing).

- **Shifts that happen in our individual interior contexts.**

Shifts in our individual interior contexts can include things like a perception of risk, fear of failure, being seen as "lacking character," unjustly accused of wrongdoing, loss of livelihood, being denied fundamental rights and liberties, being publicly humiliated, loss of control, etc. At the level of the individual interior context, there will also be childhood stories and their associated structures, themes, and narratives, as well as a story for the Heroic Mode.

Any of these factors can destabilize us and send us into high stakes, especially because, as noted earlier, childhood stories play a massive role in why we end up in high stakes.

We each respond to high stakes differently in different contexts and situations.

For some, we engage, become animated, passionate, raise our voice. In other words, it becomes very evident to ourselves and others that we are in high stakes. But this is not the only type of behavior in high stakes. For some, we withdraw and become silent — almost like the mute button has been pushed on the TV. We might even abandon the conversation by physically leaving it.

In high stakes, our behavior changes. The Actions Modes, Communication Domains, and Operating Systems that we predominantly use in low stakes can change in high stakes. Our vocal signatures also change in high stakes. A Move in Closed Power in low stakes will sound very different than a Move in Closed Power in high stakes.

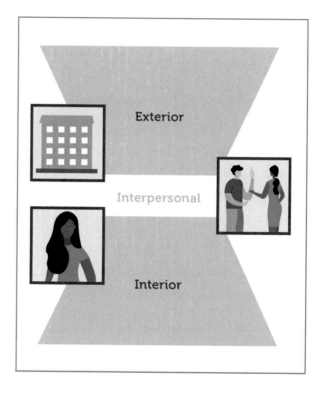

When my daughter was younger, she could easily have told you how true this is. When I remind her that it's bedtime in low stakes, it might sound like, "Let's get your teeth brushed and pajamas on — bedtime will be in 10 min."

The high-stakes version that may come after repeatedly seeing her get out of her bed and wander into the hallway will include me raising my voice and saying, "Get back in bed right this minute!" The trigger here comes from me having to repeat myself and feeling like I'm not being heard or my rules are not being respected.

For me, this evokes the high-stakes vocal signature and the behavioral change that accompanies it.

HIGH-STAKES TRIGGERS

Understanding the triggers that most likely evoke high stakes for you can offer a greater degree of psychological distance from the events as they occur.

What triggers high stakes and how we react is uniquely personal to each of us. Things that can push our buttons can include other people's styles, the voice they use in conversation, and their behavioral preferences.

EXAMPLE OF TRIGGERS

Having to interact with one's "fear opposite," or one's nemesis	Having one's feelings dismissed or belittled
Being degraded or humiliated when one can't strike back	Witnessing or experiencing loss of emotional control
Seeing someone being degraded or humiliated in public	Fear of displeasing a loved "other" or valued authority figure
Being suppressed or restrained in the freedom to act	Being subjected to the exercise of absolute authority
Having one's creativity stifled or squelched	Having one's truths or ideas prohibited or revoked
Being told one is a failure or incompetent	Being involved in or witnessing intense conflict with others
Having to engage in pseudo-intimacy	Being called shallow or superficial
Living or working with someone who habitually lies or deliberately distorts the truth	Being with people who disguise ideology as ideas
Witnessing violence, torture, or the rendering of physical harm	Being with people who are ambitious for financial gain only
Witnessing the unjust treatment of the powerless	Being with people who evidence "eccentric," "bizzare," or "freaky" behavior
Witnessing cowardice or the fear of risk	Being with people who are inauthentic or phony, or who make false claims
Betrayal of others for any personal gain	Being denied the right to be heard (feelings, ideas, solutions)
Fear of loss of control	Fear of chaos or anarchy

Reflection Time

Read through the examples of triggers above.

Which ones resonate the most with you? What makes this a trigger?

Write about the story or belief that sits behind this trigger for you.
Does it create low, medium, or high stakes?

Is there a childhood story that you can connect
to this trigger in some way?

AWARENESS OF SELF IN HIGH STAKES

Prior to developing her personal behavioral model, Trish Hallmark often felt frustrated when conflict erupted in conversations. As the stakes got higher, her ability to articulate what was happening for her became difficult. The result was that the same patterns often repeated themselves, and she felt powerless to do anything about them. "It was frustrating," she shared, looking back. "I thought it was just how I was wired."

When she eventually set out to develop a personal behavioral model, she found it difficult. At first, she found herself tipping into denial. But as she read and re-read her assessment of how she showed up in high stakes, she felt herself able to see it, define it, and own it.

Now, she describes herself as more cognizant of the impact that her reaction in high-stakes has on others. She feels more intentional with her reactions and responses, particularly in her working world. Having a defined personal behavior model has not only provided an opportunity to change and adjust in the moment, it has given her a basis for leading change in herself — finding the space to create more awareness and patience with others in high stakes moments.

"I will literally have a dialogue with myself that gives me the time to pause and evaluate another person's reaction or response, which in turn helps me with mine."

Trish Hallmark

Reflection Time

What's your behavior like when you are in high stakes?

What Action Modes (Move, Follow, Oppose, Bystand) do you use in high stakes? How is this different from low stakes?

What Communication Domains (Power, Affect, Meaning) do you use in high stakes? What brings this out for you?

What Operating Systems (Open, Closed, Random) do you use in high stakes? What brings this out?

SEEING YOUR SHADOW

When the stakes are low for us in a conversation or situation, we have access to the full range of our behavioral propensities. When the stakes are medium, we start to lose some of our range and might notice the heat rising. In high stakes, the anxiety is such that we may develop a whole different set of behaviors than we have in low stakes. At this point, we're likely operating from our "shadow." This is where our action can become reactionary, and our ability to intentionally choose our action is lessened.

As you'll recall from Juncture 4, you did some work identifying your Heroic Mode(s), becoming familiar with both their light-side "gifts" and their dark-zone "shadow" behaviors. We all have shadow behaviors, but our shadow is sometimes the part of ourselves that we like the least and are thus least likely to recognize. We can see it in others, but it's harder to recognize and accept in ourselves.

But here's the thing: ignoring our shadow only gives it more power to "run the show" and do damage. Left unexamined, it's the shadow of our Heroic Mode(s) that will believe it's right at all costs — that it has the only right way or the only right answer, and that all others are wrong.

SHADOW DANCE

In relationships that seem particularly difficult, you are likely in a situation where your shadow is dancing with someone else's shadow.

Imagine this scenario: a CEO and VP needed to work very closely together, but they were consistently challenged when it came to actually progressing on anything together. One would often say of the other, "He is so demeaning and blunt, I've never had a work relationship be so challenging and difficult." In turn, the other would say, "She leaves a wake of people behind her but is unwilling to see the devastation she creates." In meetings, the two were guarded and hesitant, carefully speaking as if tip-toeing through a room with hidden mouse traps, afraid their feet would be pinched by the traps if they stepped in the wrong place.

They were in a shadow dance with each other every time they met. One was the Protector, who had taken to the shadow behavior of the victim. They felt wronged and unjustly accused of wrongdoing. The other, the Fixer, had taken to the shadow behavior of the abuser. They gave copious amounts of feedback, yet became angry at always feeling like they had to "fix the situation."

The result was a sustained model clash. They spoke past one another constantly. Each defended their point of view by advocating that the other person needed to see it from their perspective. Neither of them ever paused the conversation long enough to actually suspend their own point of view and inquire about the other's perspective. They had given into their shadow behaviors without even realizing it — and, like anyone behaving from their shadow, they couldn't see past their belief that their own approach was the "right" approach.

Knowing your shadow

Identifying your Heroic Mode and its corresponding shadow is the first step when it comes to expanding your communicative competence and getting better results.

Getting to know our shadow means seeing the triggers that raise the stakes and set off the chain reaction that calls to the hero. It means identifying the childhood stories (and their structures) that sit behind the shadow and help us explain why we do what we do in the moment. And it means identifying the Old Internal Narrative so that we can start to write a New Internal Narrative — one that liberates us from the emotions attached to our high-stakes behavior, frees us from the shame, fear, and grief associated with our childhood stories of disappointment and betrayal, and allows us to transform the nature of our communication so it is not contaminated with our fears. Instead, this new narrative will be fed by our creative energy and help us to form and maintain better and more effective relationships.

Once you become more aware of what "high stakes" looks like for you and how you're likely to behave, you're more able to take responsibility for your shadow and have more choice in your behavior.

Locating and owning your shadow

Think of a time when you really "lost it" on someone. It might have been a boss, co-worker, client, outside stakeholder, etc. If you can't think of someone in the workplace, you can also think of other relationships in your life — a parent, spouse, sibling, child, or friend.

- What was the situation?

- Who was involved?

- What was your relationship to them?

- What was the trigger?

- What was the Heroic Mode for you?

- What do you think the Heroic Mode was for the other person?

- What is a childhood story you carry that might connect to this dynamic?

- What made this situation so explosive?

Expanding your repertoire to lower the stakes and stay out of your shadow

Observe yourself.

Over the next week, notice when the stakes start to rise for you. Make note of the context, the themes, and the triggers. What do you do in the moment?

Attend to your mindset

Attending to your mindset is important in high stakes. As long as you believe you have the power to change the situation and you are able to assume the other has a positive intent, you will be well equipped to notice when the stakes are rising and can attempt to make a change. If you believe that one or more of these things is not true, then that's the work to do first.

Practice lowering the stakes.

The best way to navigate high stakes and avoid your shadow behavior is to lower the stakes for yourself so that you can stay active and engaged in the conversation. Think of three or four strategies that work for you to help lower the stakes (e.g., ask for a brief break, count to 10, take a walk, etc.). Write these strategies down here.

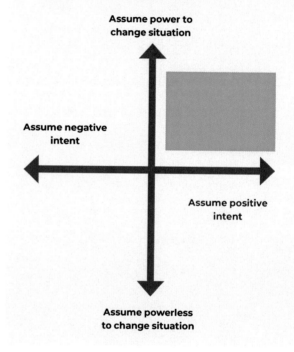

Mindset that offers the most possible outcomes

- Assume power to change situation
- Assume negative intent
- Assume positive intent
- Assume powerless to change situation

EXERCISE

Bystand in Meaning.

The ability to "bystand in meaning" is about making a neutral observation about what's happening in the moment. It can be a very effective way of saying what you're noticing about the conversation. It can also help lower the stakes for others and enable you to locate empathy for others.

It might sound like this: "It seems like we are talking past each other right now. One of us is advocating for taking action, and the other is advocating for looking at the data. I want to hear what you have to say, and I also want to be heard. Could we slow the conversation down a little bit so that we can find a meaningful outcome for both of us? Let's start with your perspective, tell me more about what you're seeing..."

Reflect on a recent high-stakes conversation. Where might you have brought in a "bystand in meaning" moment? What would it have sounded like?

Moving forward, consciously practice making a "bystand in meaning" in high-stakes conversations. When you do, return here afterward to capture your reflections.

EXERCISE

Engage in an effective cross-model conversation.

We covered the principles of cross-model conversation in Juncture 3. Once you've been able to lower the stakes for yourself and bystand in meaning, engaging in a cross-model conversation can help to further lower the stakes for you and the other person.

The bystand can be an effective way to start this two-way dialogue. It will require you to suspend any certainty you have that your way is the "right" way or the "only" way. The goal is to bring in more inquiry and less advocacy.

Reflect here on your high-stakes conversation from above. What other questions might you ask if you could re-do the conversation and initiate a cross-model conversation?

EXERCISE

Increase your tolerance for difference.

Our ability to increase our tolerance for difference is also key to lowering the stakes. This will be covered in Juncture 6. For now, just make notes of where you have judgments about the other person and their way of engaging in the moment.

Turning the moral story into a structural story

One of the best ways to gain a deeper awareness of your own behavioral patterns is to take situations that are memorable or stand out to you for some reason and use the following exercise to help turn the "moral story" into a structural story.

The **moral story** is the one you likely have with all the juicy judgment about "what a jerk" the other person was being, or why you were so in the right in the situation. Think of the moral story as the one that you call up your friend to dish about.

The structural version, by contrast, is the one that helps you really see and name what was happening in the room — without the judgment and heat. When we're able to tell the structural version, it's easier to see where we might take a different action in the future to change the outcome.

The left-hand column technique, which you've already used in this workbook, was created by Dr. Chris Argyris, professor at Harvard, as a way to help see and make sense of conversations. You can think of this as a way to Bystand on your own conversations after they have taken place. It is a way to deepen self-awareness.

Ready?

First, recall a situation that didn't go well and brought out your shadow behavior. In the right-hand column, capture the conversation exactly as it happened in the room. In the left-hand column, capture what you were thinking but not saying in the moment.

EXERCISE

For example...

Left-Hand Column	Right-Hand Column
What I'm thinking or feeling but not saying.	*What was being said.*
	Person A: Why do you think this is a good idea?
Uh...wow, I don't even think I know how to respond to that. It's clear this is not going to move forward.	**Me:** I thought it would be something that would expand our reach into this market.
	Person A: It's not a good idea right now. We have too much in our backlog to add one more thing.
Guess that's the end of that conversation. Didn't even think to ask me anything about it. We are missing a huge opportunity and this feature would actually reduce our workload. But by all means, let's keep moving and not bother to understand why someone else could possibly have anything of value to contribute.	**Me:** Okay.
	Person A: Let's move on to the next item.

EXERCISE

You can try it here.

Left-Hand Column	Right-Hand Column

Build Your Model For Leading Change

EXERCISE

Now, drawing on the skills you developed in Juncture 3 and 4 around identifying the structure of the conversation, try telling the structural story of the situation.

Reflection on Structure	Structure of the Conversation (Move, Follow, Oppose, Bystand)
I wish I had pushed back more and voiced my Oppose, rather than just saying "okay." I could have started with a Bystand to offer what I'm seeing that I don't think she's seeing, but instead I just backed away from the conversation and checked out. Next time, I will make a conscious effort to stay in the conversation and offer a Bystand. Maybe I could start by agreeing with what she said.	**Me:** Offered a Move **Person A:** Bystand **Me:** Follow **Person A:** Oppose **Me:** Follow **Person A:** Move

Now, based on seeing the structural story — reflect on the conversation further. What would it have felt like if you had voiced your perspective differently? Can you see a way that you might have bridged perspectives in order to have a cross-model conversation?

With practice and self-awareness, we enable ourselves to exercise more choice in our behaviors in the moment. Not only does this allow us to recognize where we're in high stakes and take responsibility for our shadow behavior, it helps us stay in command of our actions and behaviors so that we can get better outcomes in the moment and feel better about the interactions we have.

6 Expanding your tolerance for difference

In the previous junctures, you've explored your personal behavioral model — what it means to take responsibility for both your intent and your impact, what it looks like when you encounter someone who has a different behavioral model from you, and where model clash can trigger childhood stories and create an involuntary response that sends you into high stakes. With all of this in mind, it's time to expand your tolerance for difference.

One of the gifts of Structural Dynamics is its ability to give us a morally neutral language to name not only our own behavior, but the behavior of others in a conversation or a system. Yet being able to name something is only part of the equation. The single greatest predictor of whether our conversations will be able to generate or support change is our personal ability to grow our tolerance for people who have a different behavioral profile than our own.

Communicative competence leads to collective intelligence

One outcome of increasing your tolerance for difference is your ability to demonstrate what David Kantor calls "communicative competence."

Communicative competence is our individual ability to see the patterns in our language that are serving and not serving us, as well as to be able to bring a different language — or structure — when needed in order to change the nature of the discourse.

Communicative competence does not mean that we are perfect communicators every time, that we never reach high stakes, or that we never have an unintended impact or consequence from our actions. Rather, it means that we are able to notice when the stakes are rising and, more often than not, be more in command of ourselves in the moment when they do. We are able to stay with the conversation more productively and effectively. Moreover, we are able to assume positive intent in the other person and ask about what might be causing the response we're getting.

The indicator of reaching a higher level of communicative competence is our ability to be in dialogue and hold cross-model conversations with those that use a different language or hold a different perspective or worldview than we do.

In my experience, when leaders are charged with leading a change in an organization, the breakdown often comes on the level of communication. And,

unfortunately, we often try to fix, protect, or survive the breakdown by arguing, justifying, disengaging, abandoning, or pretending it will be fine (eventually). We look to tools, processes, policies, mandates, team-building exercises, outside consultants, changes to the organizational structure, etc. — all in an attempt to make the change more successful. But the reality of these kinds of interventions is that, even when they do "work," the solution is temporary. It is not sustainable, often lasting for just one moment in time.

The sustainable path to change lies in our ability to resolve breakdowns in our interpersonal communication dynamics through communicative competence — and our willingness to expand our tolerance for difference is key.

So, what does this require of us? It requires the willingness and ability to see the structure of the breakdown and take responsibility for our part in it. It requires us, in the moment, to suspend our judgment, locate empathy, lower the stakes, stay with the conversation, and take action to shift the nature of the conversation. These are the skills that enable us to access a group's collective intelligence — where new thinking emerges that is greater and more effective than the sum of individual thinking.

Strategies for growing your tolerance for difference

Practice expanding your tolerance for difference in low stakes first, then move to practicing in high-stakes situations. Don't start these practices with your highest-stakes conversations! This is ongoing work, and it's worth building up your skills deliberately when you are in greater command of your behavior. This is what will enable you to have more successful outcomes in the higher-stakes moments.

1. Locate empathy

Can you locate empathy for the other person? What might be going on for them? How might this conversation also be impacting them? What's the structure of the language they are using, and how might this give you insight into what they are trying to convey?

Even when you might be speaking to your "arch-nemesis," it's worth exploring how you can locate empathy for what might be happening for the other person. This "empathy doorway" opens up the path for increasing your tolerance for difference.

2. Look for sameness

While there might be lots of differences, what is something that is the same for you as it is for the other person? What is something they are saying that is also true for you — even if it's only 2 percent true?

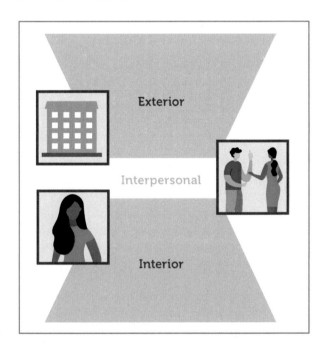

If it's difficult to find sameness in the topic of the conversation, look to a higher level of abstraction — a value that you share, an experience you share, a human condition they may be experiencing, etc. Come up out of the details in order to identify something meaningful that you share in common.

3. Expand your moral flexibility

Our inability to suspend our moral judgments about those who are "different" than us is divisive and harmful. If you have trouble locating an example of this in your workplace, just look to the broader political landscape. The United States is a country divided in half at the moment by moral certainty. The only way this will change is for us to expand our moral flexibility and inquire about other people's perspectives.

Notably, to inquire does not mean or imply agreement — it simply means being willing to be curious and wanting to understand another's perspective. It means being willing to suspend the idea that there is only one "right" viewpoint.

How tightly do you hold to your beliefs and your way of communicating? Are you able to suspend your certainty that you have the only "right" way of seeing something? Do you hold tightly to the mindset of "us vs. them"? In what situations do you see the "other" as the enemy? In what situations are you unwilling to be persuaded by empathy, data, reasoning, evidence, or threat?

4. Expand your repertoire

In Juncture 1, we explored how to expand your behavioral repertoire with the Action Modes, the Communication Domains, and the Operating Systems. Building your behavioral tool kit — especially as a means of being able to communicate more effectively with people who may use behavioral models that you are less comfortable with — is a significant way to expand your tolerance for difference.

Lean into the practice of developing a broader fluency in your language and behaviors. Notice where you have judgments, and become familiar with how your judgments may be tripping you up and causing you difficulty in your interactions with others.

4. Bystanding self in the moment

Of all the Action Modes, "Bystand" — when voiced and active — is the one action that has the greatest ability to change the nature of the discourse in the moment. Our ability in the moment to bystand ourselves (see Juncture 5) is the action of greatest awareness. It slows us down from reacting out of habit and creates the space to choose a different action.

5. Self-correct in the moment

Awareness precedes choice, precedes change — or does it? Seeing the pattern and taking responsibility for how you are contributing is Step One. But what do you do next? Lasting change happens when we are able to self-correct in the moment and interrupt our reactive habits to create a new neural pathway — a new action that changes the nature of the outcome.

Slow the pace of the conversation. Give yourself a moment to consider a different action. What's something new you might try here?

6. Know your childhood stories and their impact

We explored this work in Junctures 4 and 5. While there is a lifetime of ongoing work to unfold questions like "Where did I learn to behave like this?", knowing your stories and being able to make sense of their connections to your work today supports all of these strategies for growing your tolerance for difference.

DRAWING OUT INTOLERANCE FOR DIFFERENCE

In the abstract, it's hard to see our own judgments. But if you look back to the concept of "model clash" in Juncture 3, you'll remember that differences in vocal signatures can often draw our judgments out into the light. And drawing out where we have intolerance for difference is critical if we are to expand our tolerance for difference.

Here are a few examples of how different vocal signatures might clash:

What someone high in AFFECT might be thinking about someone high in MEANING...	What someone high in MEANING might be thinking about someone high in AFFECT...
I feel like I'm talking to a machine. This person is devoid of all emotions. They just continually talk at me, repeating all the data points over and over again. I'm not an idiot — I see the data, but the data is not the point.	This is not the time nor the place to talk about emotions. Emotions are dangerous when trying to make decisions that should be based on facts and data only.

What someone high in POWER might be thinking about someone high in MEANING...	What someone high in MEANING might be thinking about someone high in POWER...
Can we just move on? This person is constantly lost in the words and is unable to move forward on anything.	There is no regard for any context or purpose. It's just about taking an action and hoping that it meets the mark.

Build Your Model For Leading Change

Locating your intolerance for difference

Reflect on a situation where the conversation felt difficult or challenging to you in some way. Use this space to locate and draw out your judgments.

In your reflections here, you may find it helpful to refer back to the work you did in Juncture 3 on model clash and vocal signatures, as well as the work you did in Juncture 4 and 5 on childhood stories and high-stakes triggers.

Deepening Insights

The Communication Domain (Power, Affect, Meaning) is the language we choose that signals what we value or care about. What is the domain that you have the most judgment about?

- Where does the judgment come from?

- What makes it difficult to hear?

- What's the story you would tell about why your preferred domain is more useful?

- What's the connection to your childhood story?

The Operating Systems (Open, Closed, Random) are the rules we use when interacting with others. What is the Operating System you have the most judgment about?

- Where does the judgment come from?

- What makes it difficult to be in a situation where this system is the one most used?

- What's the story you would tell about why your preferred system is more useful?

- What's the connection to your childhood story?

What Communication Domain and Operating System is predominant in your work setting? Where are they similar to your own? Where is there difference? What is it like to work in systems that differ from your own preferred model? Where might this difference be a learning or growth opportunity?

Build Your Model For Leading Change

Reflection Time

From your perspective, what is important about tolerance for difference in leadership?

What are some actions you could take to expand your tolerance for difference?

How would you help others develop tolerance for difference?

7 Linking work and personal relationships

We are one human, not two separate beings. We cannot just divide ourselves in half and take one part to work while we leave the other part at home.

David Kantor referred to the work in this juncture as "optional." While highly valuable, he did not find it helpful in any way to mandate that people share work stories at home or personal stories at work. For some, there will be a clear dividing line — or even a wall — between work life and personal life. Noticing your own reaction to reading the title of this juncture, you will likely find data on your own feelings about bridging work relationships and personal relationships! What I hope this section will give you is an opportunity to consider and explore what might be possible by linking these two worlds.

This juncture has two parts to explore. Much of what we've focused on in this workbook has been work-related scenarios. So, the first part will consider how the behaviors and patterns you are seeing at work apply to your personal life as well. The second part will explore the idea of sharing parts of your behavioral model, including your childhood stories, at work.

First, let me be clear that I'm not advocating for you to walk into work tomorrow, draw your personal journey line on the board, and share everything about yourself in an all-hands meeting! That is not the point. Rather, I am advocating that you look for places where revealing more of yourself to others you work closely with might serve to deepen your relationships and improve your ability to work together.

When you are able to create enough of a trusting environment and are willing to share parts of your behavioral model — even some aspects of your childhood story — the relationship and trust-building that comes from others being able to know you a little bit deeper opens doors to higher performance and greater respect. It helps create a space where you can be seen and heard and where work feels fulfilling.

That said, there will be workplaces that do not value these levels of sharing (yet), and where it would not be safe to share. This will be a personal choice and up to you in the moment.

Trust your instincts. Know who you are sharing parts of yourself with, and consider whether you trust them enough to do so.

The link to trust in teams

In the development of teams, Alan Drexler and David Sibbett defined a model for team performance. In it, they describe core questions that every one of us has — whether consciously or unconsciously — when we come into any group or team setting.

The questions are:

- Why am I here?
- Who is here with me, who are you, and who am I?
- What are we doing?
- How will we do it?
- Who does what, when, and how?
- Why continue?

In high-performing teams, the answers to these questions are continuously being talked over and answered. When one or more of these questions goes unexplored or unanswered, the lack of clarity will start to hinder team development and performance.

The question "Who is here with me, who are you, and who am I?" is the fundamental question for trust building. While it will be helpful to know your name, where you live, and what your role is, these are surface-level answers for getting to know each other. If we apply the lens of Structural Dynamics, we might add more dimension by sharing our behavioral profiles. We could go even further by sharing elements of how we grew up and how our early experiences influence and shape our thinking today.

What's possible

In my work, I have the absolute good fortune of both witnessing the power of sharing personal stories in the workplace and watching the profound impact it can have on changing the nature of conversations in support of large-scale change.

I've watched senior leadership teams who were locked in heated debate about the direction of an org change go silent and the room be completely transformed when the most senior leader was willing to risk being vulnerable by sharing why he felt the org change was important, taking responsibility for his reactions, and sharing the source of his reactive tendencies from his childhood.

I've been in a room with a group of leaders who did not previously know one another, and watched as the energy of the room went from protection and hesitancy to vibrant fun, laughter, and connection — all because they each took a turn sharing pieces of their personal journey lines with one another.

I've experienced countless moments like this, where growth and empathy emerge on teams as a product of trust, vulnerability, and sharing.

Just as importantly, I've also had the personal joy of working with my own team of amazing people — all of whom have and continue to share their childhood stories with one another. I find that these stories deepen my sense of connection with each of them, but they also help me map and make sense of moments in which I experience dissonance between an action that's been taken and the impact it has. With a little bit of reflection, I can catch sight of what's happening and say, "Ah! This might be the place where a childhood story is showing up and high stakes are being triggered." This understanding allows me to ask about it, and we are collectively able to lower the stakes quickly and transform the conversation from breakdown to breakthrough.

Personal stories have the power to help. They help us:

- **Locate empathy**
  We can see each other as individual people with histories and emotions, not just sources of disagreement and strife.

- **Bystand in meaning**
  We can lower the stakes more quickly because we're more fully able to understand why the other person might be doing what they are doing.

- **Deepen understanding**
  We can develop a clearer understanding of each other's points of view and where our individual experiences might be playing a role in our differences.

- **Locate similarities**
  We can offer and ask for more context so that we locate similarities and shared experiences that will deepen our connection and relationship.

Reflection Time

Linking work self and personal self

Notice where there may be patterns at work that show up at home, or vice versa. Make a note of those here.

Step 1: Reflect on what you can learn from noticing these patterns.

Step 2: Reflect on how learnings from one context (home/work) may inform how you show up in the other.

Step 3: Notice what reactions you might have to the idea of disclosing personal things about your behavior with those you work with.

- Where might you push back against (or constrain) that idea?

- When might you consider doing it?

- What conditions would need to be true for you to link your work self and your personal self?

- What of this work will you share with others?

- How would it be helpful to others who are trying to understand you?

- What are you curious about in others who you work with?

Build Your Model For Leading Change

A SUMMARY OF YOUR BEHAVIORAL MODEL

Congratulations, you are well on your way to defining your personal behavioral model!

By deep-diving your relationship to the 4 Levels of Behavior and expanding your awareness of your behavioral dynamics through the 7 Junctures of Functional Self-Awareness, you have begun the imperative journey of discovering, defining, and expanding your own behavioral model.

Models take different forms for each person. Some people draw diagrams, some write books, some write a one-page summary, and others write pages upon pages. You cannot get this wrong or do it wrong. What's important is the insight and meaning-making this process gives you in order to turn your insights into behavior changes.

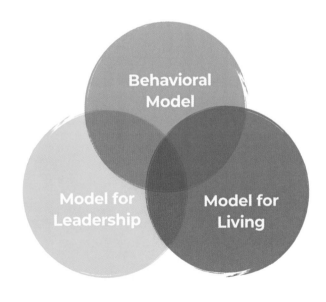

The point is that you have started — and will continue to do the thinking — and the thinking brings more and more clarity over time.

Behavioral Model Summary

As you continue to refine your behavioral model, here are some of the key features that you are now able to clearly articulate for yourself and others. Capture a summary of what you want to remember here.

My behavior in low stakes is...

My behavior in high stakes is...

For me, the feeling of high stakes is triggered by themes like...

The actions that are the most dominant for me are...

The actions that I'm working on developing are...

The behavior that challenges me the most in others is...

The behavior I am noticing has negative impacts on others is...

EXERCISE

My vocal signature in high stakes is...

My Heroic Mode(s) is/are...

My "light" zone is...

My "shadow" zone is...

My childhood story is...

My Old Internal Narrative is...

Let go of who you think you're supposed to be; embrace who you are.

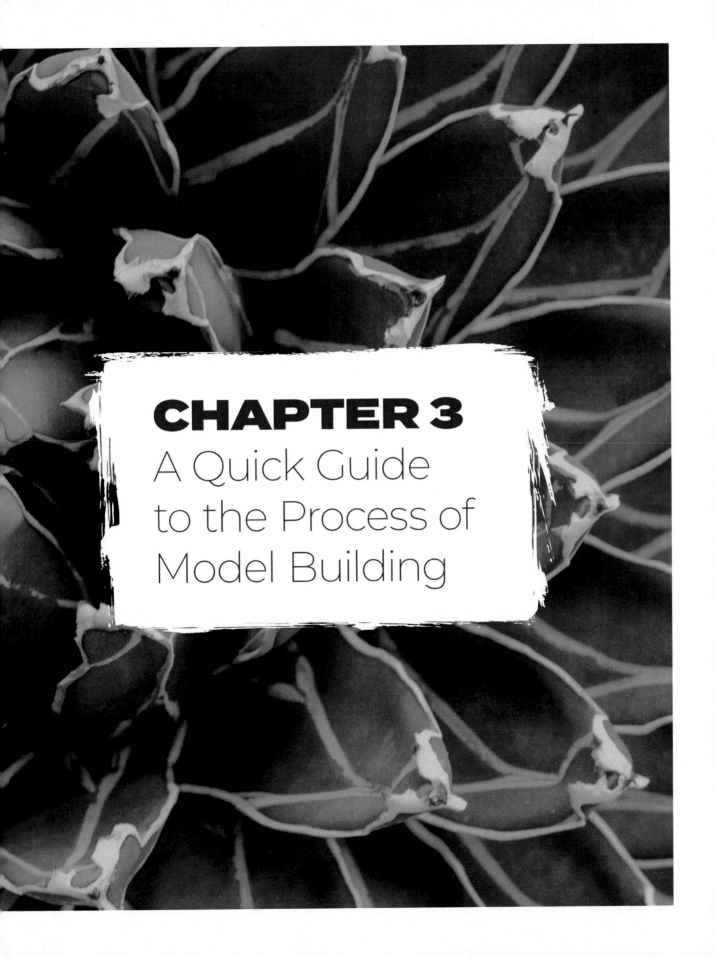

CHAPTER 3
A Quick Guide
to the Process of
Model Building

Build Your Model For Leading Change

THE PROCESS OF MODEL BUILDING

In the last two chapters, you worked to uncover your behavioral model, a process of building your awareness (and expanding your repertoire) around the beliefs and behaviors you bring with you into every interaction and relationship.

In this chapter, you will now begin the process of building models to help you lead and live with a similarly high level of awareness and intentionality.

Model building is the (ongoing, never done) process of making the implicit more explicit. Most of us have reasons for why we do what we do, but we often take our reasons at face value.

We don't explore why we do what we do, our reasons just feel like tacit knowledge or received wisdom. And this, of course, makes our actions harder for us to learn from.

Our model is the why behind what we do. It is our thinking, our reasons, and our actions. When we make these explicit, it creates clarity for us and those around us.

To paraphrase my colleague Antoinette Coetzee, you can't change what you can't name.

There are endless models in our world: models for how teams develop, how organizations change, how individual change happens. There are models for agility in teams and organizations, models for leadership, models for intervention... the list goes on.

All of these models are useful in helping us make sense of the world around us — but they all have their flaws. As the late David Kantor (the author of the theory of Structural Dynamics and Model Building) said, the only wrong model will be the one that asserts it's the only way.

GRAB YOUR PEN!

The exercise below is designed for you to take a moment to jot down the specific kinds of models you are aware of, as well as whether and how you use them. Think of this as an inventory to draw from as you explore what you're already doing, what you would like to do better or differently, and what kinds of resources you have at your fingertips.

MY INVENTORY OF MODELS

Take a few minutes to pause and capture some models that you are aware of — and perhaps even use to some degree in your daily life.

- What's the name of the model?
- What's the purpose of the model?
- Who is the author?
- Where did you learn about it?
- Did you have a mentor?
- What do you find useful about it?
- What do you find less useful?
- Do you **explicitly** share with others that you are using it? Or is it a more **implicit** model that informs how you think and work but that you keep to yourself?

Model	Purpose	Author

Build Your Model For Leading Change

Chances are, you will be able to fill in the inventory below with at least a few examples of models you've either used, seen in action, or are generally aware of.

Great! These will give you a solid framework for exploring where you are in the 3 stages of Model Building in the following pages.

Mentor	Useful	Less Useful	Explicit/Implicit

THE 3 STAGES OF MODEL BUILDING

David Kantor, who founded the theory of Structural Dynamics, identified and defined three core stages of model building:

- **Imitation**

- **Constraint**

- **Autonomy**

I like to start with these three stages because it's helpful to be able to identify where you are when you're learning something new and trying to make sense of it as you apply it.

Stage 1: Imitation

In the Imitation stage, we are proactively seeking to understand the world by learning about other models. We read, seek mentorship, and look for programs that help us understand ourselves and our interactions with others.

Let's imagine that you're coaching a team and your primary model for team development is Tuckman's Stages of Team Development — Forming, Storming, Norming, and Performing. You use this all the time with teams, it's how you think about engaging with a team, you reference it during team meetings often, and you're quick to explain the model to others when you think it's appropriate or useful. This is the space of Imitation.

When we're in this stage of model building, we are "imitating" others who have used or developed this model. We're not really thinking about what

we would change about the model. We're just trying to learn it and use it as its author intended.

This is a period of experimentation, but not innovation. While in this stage, you might try out the model by using it in different scenarios or settings. It's like you're trying it on — like you would a new pair of shoes, deciding if they really fit or not.

As humans, we imitate what others are doing — although sometimes with less skill than we might desire — in order to internalize and apply what we're learning. This is exactly what this stage of model building is all about.

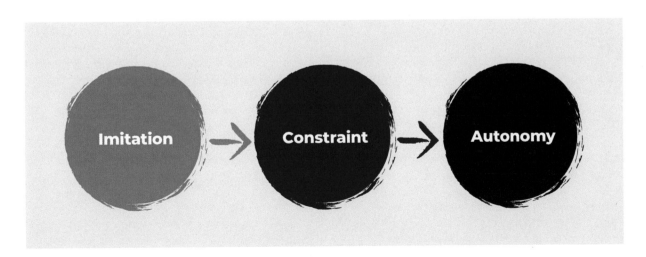

Stage 2: Constraint

Stage 2 reflects the fact that we inevitably start to test the limits of whatever model we're using while in the space of Imitation. We find things that resonate for us deeply and other things that don't.

In the stage of constraint, we start to question whether the model we've been using is doing everything we want it to. This is the stage of sifting and sorting a model's assumptions, beliefs, and actions in ways that do or don't answer your needs. You might find yourself saying things like:

- "Keep this"
- "Discard that"
- "Re-shape it to do this"
- "Invent something new to do that"

Drawing from the example above, imagine that you start to sense a shift in your use of the Tuckman model for team development. Initially, it had taken such a prominent role in all your work — it was great! But now you've read some research that suggests that it may not work like it was originally intended to. The linear phases are not done in set periods of time, for example, and you've actually experienced teams that never seem to leave the Storming phase but who nevertheless get work done. Over time, you find yourself starting to question the model and pushing back on the idea.

You've now entered the phase of Constraint. You're challenging and pushing back on the model. You've decided you like keeping the phrases — Forming, Norming, Storming, and Performing — but you're ready to bring in more. In fact, you've discovered another team model you really like called the Drexler Sibbet Team Performance Model. The theory under this model is that a team can be in multiple places at every given moment in time. This resonates more for you and reflects what you've experienced with your team. So you decide you're going to keep the phrases of one model, discard the details of it, and re-shape it by layering it on top of another model.

This stage of model building is inevitable, because all models have their limitations. As you begin to explore ways that a model is incomplete or breaks down in certain circumstances, you are "constraining" it. And in Kantor's theory of model building, he sees this as a natural progression — one we must do if we're truly going to get to the place of having our own model.

When you constrain a model, you will be doing so from the lens of your own experience and, therefore, your own developing personal model. When something creates dissonance, it's an opportunity to inquire, reflect, and be curious. It becomes an opportunity to engage in a cross-model conversation with someone else, and it is an essential step to building your own model.

Constraint offers both an opportunity to reflect and an invitation to incorporate new thinking. It is, simultaneously, expanding our personal model and our tolerance for difference.

CAPTURE YOUR THINKING!

Because this is such a crucial phase of developing your own model, I'm offering the following grid for you to use along your journey. Wherever you find yourself starting to Constrain a model, use this space to consider what you might keep with you, what you might discard or leave behind, and what you might want to re-shape or invent to better meet your needs.

Model-Building Reflections

Here is a sample

Topic/Model: _____

Keep	Re-Shape
Discard	Invent

Stage 3: Autonomy

In the phase of Autonomy, we start to incorporate the selected parts of other (imitated) models into our own. We are no longer "borrowing" other models — we have our own model that is developed enough for others to Imitate and Constrain.

In this stage, you're at the place where you may use parts of the Tuckman model, parts of the Drexler Sibbet model, and parts of several other models. But the key is that these various parts are wholly encompassed into your own model.

You know how you work with teams, you know why you do what you do, and you know where your thinking is sourced from. You honor those thought leaders who have come before you and appreciate their thinking because it has shaped and shifted your own. Their thinking has helped guide you in the development of a team model that is all your own.

But, most importantly, when you are clear about why you do what you do when working with teams, it provides you with a grounded confidence for when things go upside down in teamwork. In fact, In this phase, you are so clear about what you do and why that you could teach your model to others.

THEORIZING AN EFFECTIVE MODEL

When we start talking about a conceptual thing like "my professional model" or "my model for leadership," it can easily become overwhelming. It's easy to get turned around. You might even start to question how you can get started when you don't already know what your model is.

But here's the thing: I would suggest that you already have a model for leadership (and likely other models, as well), you just might not have thought about it in these terms and you might not have taken the time to make your model explicit.

The practice of model building requires each of us to embark on a lifelong learning process. To believe that no model is perfect — that they will all have their limitations — frees us up to learn and explore. And the more we learn and practice, the clearer we get about what works for us and why. Moreover, when we encounter people who have a different model from ours, the "cross-model conversations" that emerge can help us get even more clear on our thinking. Because seeing different models in action presents a choice: we do not have to operate from the same model, but we can talk about our differences and explore what might work best for us moving forward.

The space of ongoing exploration, reflection, and practice involved in model building is captured by David Kantor when he suggested that a complete model has four major components:

- **The theory of the "thing"** — What's the focus or subject of your model? (In this section of the workbook, the "thing" is *leadership*; in Chapters 1 and 2, the "thing" was *personal behavior*; and in Chapter 5, as you'll see, the "thing" is *living.*)

- **The theory of change** — How do you believe that change is brought about within or for the "thing" that you are focusing on? (For example, how do you believe people can change or grow their leadership behavior? How do you believe that personal behavior change can happen? How do you believe that behavior change can happen in teams and in organizations?)

- **The theory of practice** — What do you believe about what you should do, based on your understanding of the "thing" and how it changes? (For example, if you want to change your behavior in relation to the "thing," how would you go about doing that? What steps, in theory, would you be taking? What steps would you take to change how you show up as a leader? What steps do you believe would be most effective to make your own behavior change happen?)

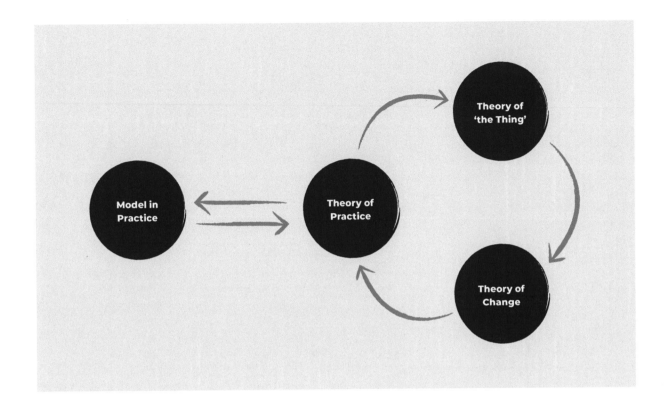

- **The model in practice** — Life never goes exactly as planned. There is your "theory" of what you would do, and then there is what you *actually* do "in the room" to make a change in relation to the "thing" at the heart of your model. (For example, if you are taking steps to change your behavior based on your theory of practice, your model in practice is where you see and engage with the bigger picture of how your own behavior shifts in relation to external dynamics and the specific needs of what you encounter in the "real world.")

The goal of setting up these four components of a complete model is to define, clarify, and refine our understanding of what the topic is, what we want to achieve when we set out to change or address it, what we believe about how change should happen, what we believe about ourselves and others in the room, and what we might actually do in the moment.

In other words, it's about deeply exploring the topic, the goals, our desired behavior and outcomes, and our actual behavior and how it affects the potential outcomes. It's about exploring all these things from every different angle and developing a robust model that truly works with us and for us.

Why so many theories?

There is often a gap between the reasons we give for our actions and how we actually behave. This is what Chris Argyris refers to as "espoused theory" versus "theory in use." In model building, the goal is to focus on a very specific "thing" so that you can refine your thinking and your practice and be really clear on what you're trying to achieve.

For example, when you picked up this book, you likely had a definition of "change" in mind. What was it? What did you want to change?

When we use a broad and general term like "change," we might just be thinking that we don't like the current situation and we want it to be better. But have you really stopped to think about what, exactly, it is that you want to change and what that change would look like?

This is why Kantor has us start with the "theory of the 'thing.'" We really need to know what we're focused on.

Let's explore this a little further: a leader in a formal leadership role may have just been tasked with improving performance in their division. She might know that a change is needed, but beyond the goal of "improvement" and "producing a better outcome," does she know what would need to change to make that happen? Likely, this leader could use a model for leadership, a model for leading organizations, and a model for "leader as interventionist."

Why so many models? Because change is complex, and very seldom does a performance improvement happen just by changing a process. The leader in this example will need a way of making sense of team dynamics, their own role in the dynamic, their power and authority as a leader, an understanding of human systems, and a way to look at behavior. These are each models that, if articulated, can help her focus on the thing that needs changing and on her practice of leading a team toward that change.

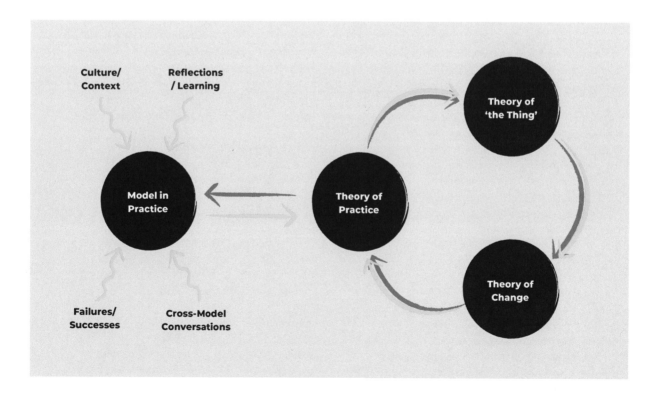

WHY CAN'T WE JUST HAVE A PRACTICE?

A practice is, in itself, developed from two phenomena: the *theory* of practice (how a leader *thinks* she should be and what she believes she should do) and her *model in practice* (what she actually does in practice, in the room).

When your theory of practice — how you believe you should be in the room and what you think you should do in the room — meets the constraint of your organization's culture, human dynamics, and pushback from others, this is where your *model in practice* comes into play. How do you actually show up in these moments? How does your theory work/evolve/deviate in response to the reality of the dynamics you encounter?

In the moment, when things fall out of alignment between theory and practice, you might engage in cross-model conversations that change your thinking. Or later, your reflective journaling practice might reveal new insights to learn from. All of these feed back into your evolving theory of practice, which may inform new changes that you would like to make in your *model in practice*.

It's an ongoing cycle of defining and refining, and it's facilitated by having clearly theorized the "thing" you need to focus on, your theory of change, and your theory of practice. These all inform your practice model.

Are you ready?

As David Kantor points out, you can apply this framework to develop any professional model. For example:

- Leadership

- Leading Change

- Agile Team Coaching

- Leadership Coaching

- Organizational Transformation

But here, in the next several chapters of this workbook, we'll be focusing on building a model for leadership, a model for living, and a model for leading change. Along with deeply understanding your personal behavioral model (Chapters 1 and 2), these are the most important models you can develop if you want to *lead change* in a sustainable way moving forward.

Are you ready? The reflection questions and prompts I have provided in the following chapters will help you formulate your model for leading change — no matter where your journey brings you.

A JOURNEY OF PROFESSIONAL MODEL BUILDING

At first, Antoinette Coetzee wasn't convinced that she understood what a professional model was. For her, she's been working toward developing her team coaching model. But she was struggling. She had collected all sorts of models and pieces of models that were not explicit in her practice. But, she now says, "you can't manage something if you can't language it."

For Antoinette, being able to "language it" means being able to name what you're doing and why you're doing it. Before she articulated her model, she found herself flying by the seat of her pants. Sometimes things worked, sometimes they didn't, but she never felt fully sure why it would go one way or the other. It created a lot of self-doubt and anxiety.

Now, having developed her model for team coaching, Antoinette is able to articulate her model and enrolll team members into a process that they understand and that feels authentic. She is able to enrolll them into their own process for change.

Her model, she shares, has given her the feeling of choice.

"It grounds me and gives me more possibilities. It enables me to bring clarity for others. It makes it possible to see gaps. It makes it possible to say no."

Antoinette Coetzee

CHAPTER 4
How to Develop YOUR Model for Leadership

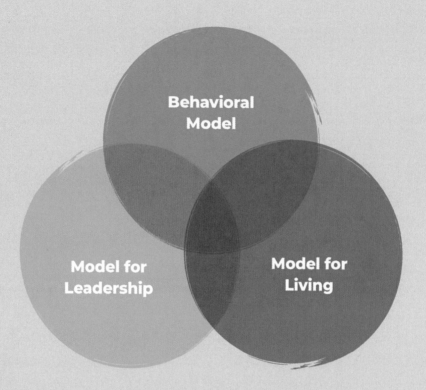

If you want to lead change in a meaningful way, the core model you need to develop is your model for leadership — and you have already taken the first critical step of the process by exploring your behavior model. You have already started to develop the deep and personal knowing of self that forms the basis of any version of effective leadership.

Now, one could make a career of studying and learning the different models of leadership that exist in our world. However, while all these models may be helpful and certainly serve to inspire and provoke our thinking, here's what I know to be true:

The most profound shift we can make as leaders of ourselves and others is when we are ready to undertake the creation of our own leadership model.

In this chapter, you will be developing your model for leadership using the four components of model building discussed in Chapter 3

The theory of the "thing" — What's the focus or subject of your model?

The theory of change — How do you believe that change is brought about within or for the "thing" that you are focusing on?

The theory of practice — What do you believe about what you should do, based on your understanding of the "thing" and how it changes?

The model in practice — Life never goes exactly as planned. There is your "theory" of what you would do, and then there is what you actually do "in the room" to make a change in relation to the "thing" at the heart of your model.

Model for Leadership:
The Theory of the "Thing"

Building your model for leadership will require you to reflect on the theory of leadership, which is the "thing" that your model is focusing on.

The purpose of the following reflections is to help you get to the definitive aspects of what leadership is to you. How do you define leadership? What does it mean to you?

The next set of questions might feel obvious to you, but you might be surprised to find that others see leadership differently! Keep reflecting, even if things feel obvious — this is where the deep clarity of self-aware leadership begins.

What does leadership mean to you?

Over the decades, we have collectively defined leadership in many different ways. From the early definitions of the "Great Man" theory suggesting that leaders are simply born to more modern definitions of leadership that frame it as a way of being, acting, and taking responsibility for yourself and your impact on others. In this more modern definition, we believe that leaders are made, not born.

Leadership is an endless field of study and theory. The field is so vast that it can be hard to find a place to start. Here, I'll offer one frame for thinking about leadership as a way to prime your thinking.

Grady McGonagill wrote an Annotated Bibliography on Leadership suggesting that there are generally four theories of leadership that can be viewed on a two-by-two matrix of implementation focus and approach.

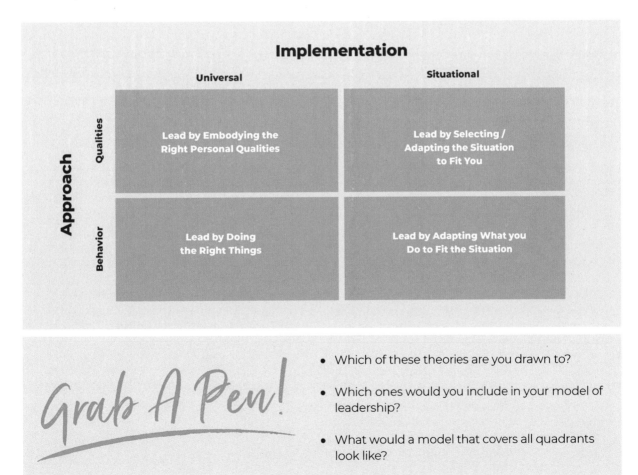

- Which of these theories are you drawn to?

- Which ones would you include in your model of leadership?

- What would a model that covers all quadrants look like?

FURTHER EXPLORATION

Here are some specific examples of existing leadership models that focus on leaders embodying certain personal qualities:

- Jim Collins, in his book *Good to Great*, defines the essential ingredient of leadership as a person who blends personal humility with intense professional will and demonstrates characteristics like humility, will, ferocious resolve, and giving credit to others.

- Stephen Covey, in his book *Principle-Centered Leadership*, argues that leadership should be guided by defined principles (e.g., continually learning, service orientation, radiating positive energy).

- Daniel Goleman, in his book *Emotional Intelligence: Why it Matters More than IQ*, identified five components of emotional intelligence: self awareness, self regulation, motivation, empathy, and social skill.

- Bill Joiner and Steve Josephs, in their book *Leadership Agility: Five Levels of Mastery for Anticipating and Initiating Change,* argue that differences in the quality of thinking make a difference in how leaders approach challenging situations. Their work builds on the work of Bill Torbert and Robert Kegan.

- Robert Kegan, in his book *In Over Our Heads: The Mental Demands of Modern Life*, presents a theory of leadership that says leaders develop in stages of adult development. The higher the stage of development, the better equipped we are to deal with modern complex challenges.

Another set of existing leadership models focuses on leading by doing the right thing:

- Ronald Heifetz, in his book *Leadership Without Easy Answers*, talks about how leaders can respond by mobilizing people to tackle tough problems (adaptive challenges) differently than they tackle more simple issues (technical problems). He introduces specific principles, starting with "getting on the balcony."

- Bill Isaacs, in his book *Dialogue and the Art of Thinking Together*, says that the capacity to foster group dialogue is an essential skill for leaders because it taps into the inherent wisdom in the field, which is accessible through collective intelligence.

- Doug Stone and Sheila Heen, in their book *Difficult Conversations*, talk about a critical interpersonal skill of leadership being the ability to engage in "learning conversations."

- David Kantor, in his book *Reading the Room*, defines communicative competence as an essential skill for leadership, suggesting that it essentially "defines" the leader, and that behavioral change happens through positive and negative feedback loops in the system.

The following models focus on leading by adapting what you do to fit the situation:

- Daniel Goleman, in the book *Primal Leadership*, talks about how a leader's mood greatly impacts others and how their primary task is to manage their mood to establish a positive environment.

- Ken Blanchard, in the book *Leadership and the One Minute Manager*, outlines a model for situational leadership where different situations require different kinds of leadership — directing, coaching, supporting, or delegating.

- Karen and Henry Kimsey-House, in their book *Co-Active Leadership*, define leadership as harnessing the power of the collective. Based on the situation, you can access one of five dimensions of leadership: leading from the front, from behind, from beside, from within, or from the field.

And the final group of models below focuses on leading by adapting the situation to fit you:

- Robert Greenleaf, in his book *Servant Leadership*, says that there are great leaders and servant leaders who are attuned to the needs and voices of others. He places an emphasis on developing personal qualities as a leader.

- F. Fiedler, in A *Theory of Leadership Effectiveness*, offers the "contingency theory": that the effectiveness of a leader's style fits the context.

These are just four lenses and some of the hundreds of models available on leadership. There are certainly more worth exploring: working with shadow behaviors or heroic modes, for example. In Structural Dynamics, we look at the importance of childhood stories and how they play a critical role in regulating our behavior as adults. We also look at the ethics of leadership, systemic leadership, and sustainability.

Leadership Model Building

React to the theories that you've just read about. Make notes about what you would keep, re-shape, discard and invent in your model.

Model-Building Reflections

Topic/Model: **LEADERSHIP**

Keep	Re-shape
Discard	Invent

NOTES

Deep Diving Existing Models

Pick 1–2 books — maybe one that I mentioned earlier or another leadership book that you're curious about — and take a deep dive into the model. Make notes about the essence of each of these theories.

- How do they define leadership?

- What is their theory of how change happens?

- What are leaders doing?

Title _____

Author _____

Notes

Title _____

Author _____

Notes

Reflection Time

Use these questions below to capture insights and reflections about what you're learning. In the notes space on the following pages, respond to these from your perspective — how would you answer these questions for yourself?

- What are the specific characteristics, actions, and beliefs that define leadership?

- Which type of leadership theories are you most drawn to?

- How would you identify good or effective leadership in others? What behaviors do they demonstrate?

- What kinds of leadership do you admire and why?

- What examples of leadership turn you off and why? What specific behaviors are these individuals exhibiting?

NOTES

NOTES

Defining Moments

We all have defining moments — those moments you vividly remember — that were likely a little (or a lot) difficult and that grew you as a person and a leader. I call these "defining moments of leadership."

Inspiration Time!

What defining moments or experiences of your own life have shaped your definition of leadership?

What did these moments teach you about your own leadership?

Capture your stories and reflections here.

 For inspiration, check out my podcast Defining Moments of Leadership, where I explore real-life moments with real leaders. We talk about the lessons that grew them and defined what leadership means to them.

Summarizing Leadership

Using your explorations from above, make notes about the following aspects of leadership that are important to you.

What are the principles that define leadership?

What moral values must a leader possess?

What are the skills that define effective leadership for you?

Model for Leadership:
Theory of Change

The theory of change articulates how your model understands the nature of change. What brings change about? What are the prerequisites for it to happen?

In Structural Dynamics, the theory of change holds the following to be true:

- Change is systemic in nature

- Behavior is regulated by positive and negative feedback loops

- Context matters

- Underlying structures, both visible and invisible, are always present in a room and impact our individual and collective decisions about behavior

There are other theories of change, too. For example, *social constructionism* says that we create our own reality through the words and metaphors we use and the conversations we have — and that this drives our behavior. *Heliotropic hypothesis* holds that social systems evolve toward the most positive images they have of themselves and that to change the system we have to change the shared image.

The goal here is to explore your theory for change so that this can inform your developing understanding of your model for leadership and how you can lead change productively and with intention.

Reflection Time

In this section, you will explore how you believe leaders get better — how they grow their leadership. How do leaders bring about the changes that they desire in themselves and others?

In the pages to come, think about what you are trying to change, and then answer some or all of the following questions.

- What are you trying to change, specifically?

- How do you believe change happens?

- How do you bring about change in another person?

- Do you take a systemic view of change? Why or why not?

- How do you help others become better at leadership or become better leaders?

- Through what stages does someone evolve their leadership?

- How can a leader sustain newly developed thinking or behavior?

- Is there a consistent process that leads to change?

- How does context — time, place, and person — affect how change happens?

- What is the goal of better leadership?

NOTES

NOTES

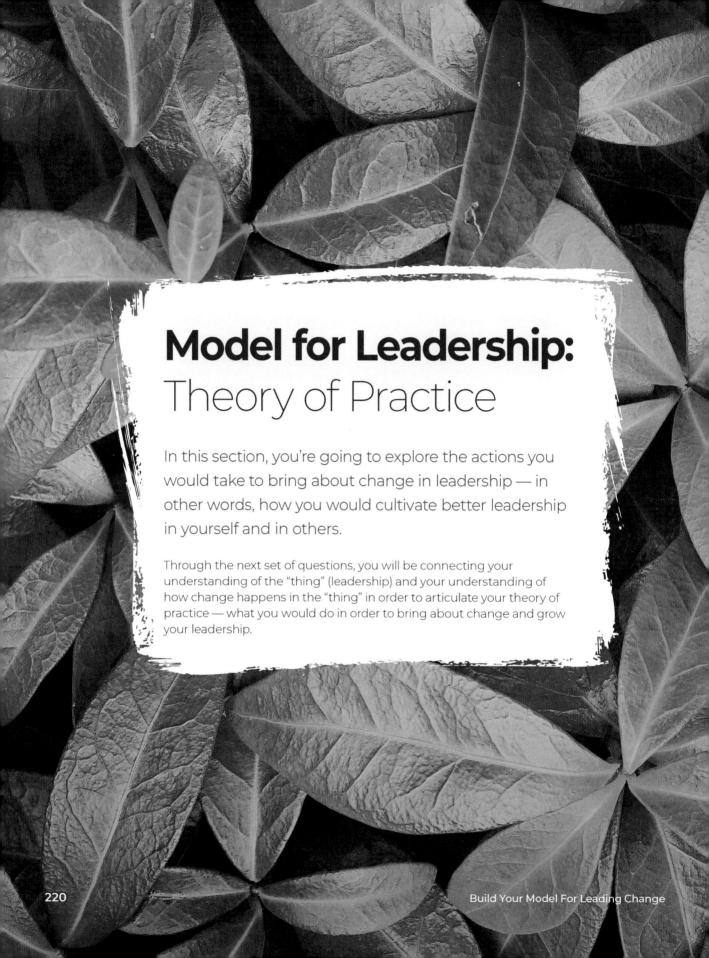

Model for Leadership:
Theory of Practice

In this section, you're going to explore the actions you would take to bring about change in leadership — in other words, how you would cultivate better leadership in yourself and in others.

Through the next set of questions, you will be connecting your understanding of the "thing" (leadership) and your understanding of how change happens in the "thing" in order to articulate your theory of practice — what you would do in order to bring about change and grow your leadership.

Reflection Time

Reflecting on your theory of what effective leadership looks like, how would you go about learning, developing, and expanding these traits in your leadership?

What are your leadership goals? Where do you place your attention and focus?

What do you want to be known for? In other words, what would you want someone to say about you if they were describing you to someone else?

Reflection Time

What specific tools, techniques, and practices can help you develop the leadership characteristics you want to be known for? (In other words, what specific tools, techniques, and practices will help you grow your leadership?)

What specific tools, techniques, and practices help you grow leadership?

What structures will you put in place for feedback about your leadership?

NOTES

Model for Leadership:
Your Model in Practice

The final step to building your model for leadership is putting all the theories into action.

Your model in practice is the most visible and accessible part of model building. For some, they put this model out for anyone to read and see. Pick up any nonfiction book about leadership, team development, or agile transformation and you will be reading about and seeing the author's model in practice. For others, their model in practice may be held closely. Either way is fine — after all, this process is about defining and refining YOUR model in a way that is clear and accessible for YOU.

Your model in practice is highly informed by your theory of practice and having explored the specific tools, techniques, principles, sequenced steps and practices that you believe will help bring growth and change in your leadership. But what's unique is that your model in practice changes when your theory meets other human beings! In every context or situation, you may find yourself adapting to the constraints that exist in that system. And as the gap between your espoused theory (theory of practice) and your theory in use (your model in practice) grows, there will be plenty of opportunities for reflection and adaptation as needed.

> Are you ready to engage with some ~ questions to kickstart your exploration of your model in practice?

YOUR LEADERSHIP SKILLS INVENTORY

In your "Model for Leadership: Theory of the Thing," you defined the skills of effective leadership. List those identified skills below.

Next, on a scale of 0 to 10, score how effective you believe you are in each of these skills today. Make notes about which skills you are actively working on, which ones you feel you are already skillful in, and which ones you feel like are more aspirational for you at the moment.

Then, reflect on what's coming up for you in the next 6 months. Which of these skills will serve you best, given the context and what's coming? For these skills, enter the rating you would like to have achieved in 6 months.

Creating accountability: Make an appointment in your calendar for 6 months from today and note this page number in the workbook. Then, when the time comes, remember to come back and check in on how you're doing!

My Leadership Skills	Current score on a scale of 0–10	Desired score in 6 months on a scale of 0–10
Ex: Communicative competence	5	8

Reflection Time

How do you bring your leadership to life in the room? What actions do you take?

In everyday practice, how do you grow leadership in teams? In others?

What are the principles that inform your work on a daily basis?

Looking at the Model Building Inventory you developed earlier in this workbook, which (if any) of these practice models inform your own? Did you read about them or learn them from someone else?

What role do ethics play in your leadership?

What role does moral integrity play in your leadership?

How do you get regular feedback on the impact of your leadership on others?

DEEPEN THE WORK

Perhaps more than any other aspect of model building, the potential gaps between your theory of practice and your model in practice can be challenging in the moment. That's why these gaps are particularly rich territory for the ongoing reflective journaling practice discussed in the beginning of this workbook.

To explore these gaps, try out the methods of reflecting before and reflecting after.

Reflecting before offers the opportunity to set your intentions around your theory of change and your theory of practice in relation to the theory of the "thing."

- What is it that you are focused on?

- What do you believe about how change will happen?

- What tools, techniques, and practices will help bring growth and change?

Reflecting after provides you with the opportunity to explore your model in practice.

- How did you bring your leadership to life in the room?

- What actions did you take?

- How did it go?

While this is the ongoing work of reflective journaling, I've offered two columns below to get you started.

Reflecting before	Reflecting after

MY MODEL FOR LEADERSHIP IN SUMMARY

Model building is ongoing work. You will continue to refine your model for leadership over time, but here are some of the key features that you are now able to clearly articulate for leading yourself and others. Capture a summary of what you want to remember here.

Leadership is…

What people can expect from me is…

What I ask of others is…

I am the kind of leader who…

I believe that...

I am celebrating these wins...

I am learning from these low moments...

My growth edge is...

Reflection Time

Reflections on Your Model

Now that you have something on paper, journal about your experience of defining your model. What was it like? What was easy? What did you find more difficult?

Constraint and Gaps

All models are helpful and also have their limitations. Make note of gaps or places that you want to continue to grow or refine.

Build Your Model For Leading Change

NOTES

You know all of those things you've always wanted to do?

You should go do them.

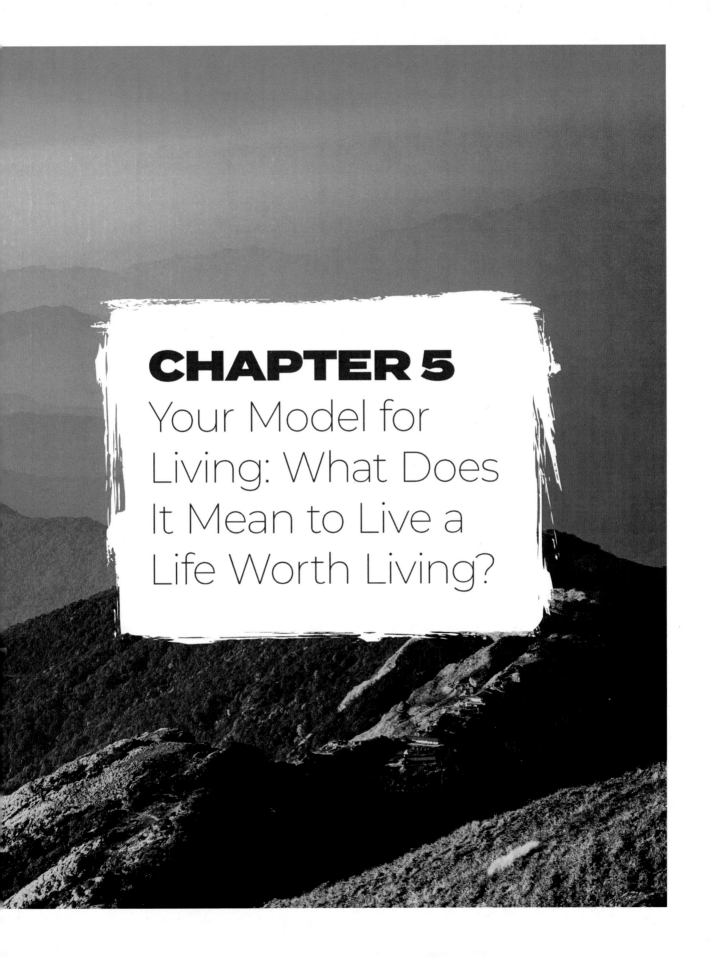

CHAPTER 5

Your Model for Living: What Does It Mean to Live a Life Worth Living?

DO YOU "LIVE TO WORK" OR "WORK TO LIVE"?

What does it mean to balance work life and home life?

These are pressing questions for all of us, and when it comes to balance, it's rarely an easy answer. How we think about work-life balance — much less how we implement our thinking into our day-to-day actions — is unique to each and every one of us.

But, as you've likely experienced at some point in your life, it's easy to put on cruise control and not take the time to really consider what our individual ideal balance might look like in our lives — what it might feel like, what it would take to achieve, and what impact it would have on our well-being.

This chapter invites you to take the time. Here. Now.

Furthermore, I argue that you have to take the time if you are truly serious about building a model for leading change.

Your model for living gives you an important lens through which to view your model for leadership — which, as I've argued before, is the crucial framework for being able to lead change. Your model for living helps to constrain and support your model for leadership by clearly articulating the things outside your professional life that matter most.

As a quick example: in my model for leadership, I know that I value personal connections and creating space for the leaders I'm coaching. In my model for living, I know that I value time with my family. By being clear about both of these models — what I value, why, and how I intend to shape my interactions based on these values — I am able to create boundaries with my coaching clients: I won't take calls after 4:30pm on Monday through Friday. In this example, my model for living and my model for leadership inform each other — I know that because I value family time there will be less time for coaching clients. I'm willing to say no when those requests are made. But I may also choose to intentionally and thoughtfully make exceptions to my rule on occasion — often by making sure that the exception is for a limited time only and because I know it will have a clear and positive impact for my client.

Here's another example: part of my model for living is that I want to live in a way that brings me joy (here's looking at you, Marie Kondo!). This value has direct bearing on my model for leadership, in that to say "yes" to any work (partnership, workshop, coaching engagement, etc), it needs to be work that brings me joy with people that bring me joy. If not, it's not a good fit. When I pay attention to "fit," I show up differently. My attitude is different. I have more patience, and I just perform better overall. On the occasions where I've said "yes" even knowing that it was not a good fit, I have regretted the decision each and every time. While in the moment it might seem like a good idea — often it is not.

In other words, your models for leading change really do form a Venn diagram. It's all connected. Building a clear model for living — one informed by your values — and

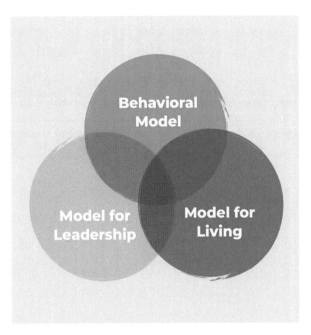

understanding how it informs your model for leadership and your personal behavioral model is a critical facet of being able to lead change:

- You know who you are

- You know how you communicate

- You know what you value

- You know what you believe about leadership

This is how you prepare to lead meaningful, sustainable change.

For those of us (I'm included in this group) who have a tendency to put others first and ourselves last (or not at all) this chapter is for you! The model for living helps to constrain being out of alignment with what we value personally and professionally.

WHERE LIFE AND LEADERSHIP COME TOGETHER

The 2020 global COVID pandemic was a huge systemic intervention that disrupted life as we knew it. Many of us were forced to look at our relationship to work and life through a new lens. For others, the pandemic forced us to really follow through on some of the thinking we'd been circling around for quite some time.

Questions like:

- What are my boundaries between work and home?

- What's important to me?

- Where do I want to prioritize my time?

- What does a life well lived look like?

- Who am I *being* when I'm living my best life?

- What am I *doing* when I am living my best life?

These are questions that we all need to be asking.

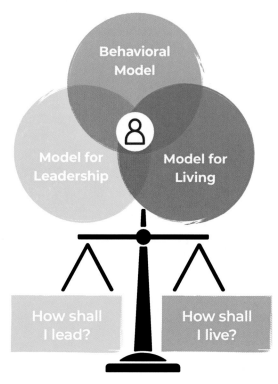

But why would you take the time to explore these questions in a workbook on leading change? What could they possibly have to do with leading change on teams and in organizations?

Simple: if you've ever had the experience of feeling overworked, exhausted, burnt out, angry that your weekend time is infused with work tasks, or like you're taking meetings during your dinner hour almost every night, then chances are you're experiencing a leadership model that is out of balance or integrity with your model for living.

Our emotions are our guidance system. Joy, sadness, anger, frustration, fear ... these feelings are data! Don't ignore them! They are signals to check-in with ourselves and be curious (rather than judgmental) about what's happening and where we might be out of integrity with our model for living.

Here's an example: a leader who values connection time with his family feels angry about working over weekends. His personal value of family connection is being "stepped on" by work. Notably, he is simultaneously being driven by a childhood story that stops him from pushing back at work and saying "no" because he fears he will not be seen as a team player and may ultimately be fired. Left unexamined and unchecked over a period of time, the anger continues to build and eventually he finds himself in high stakes most of the time. Then, unprovoked, he has an angry outburst directed at his boss one evening. To his boss, it felt like it came out of nowhere. The result? He lost his job.

So, yes, emotions help us know when a value we hold is being stepped on. But if you've never done the work to define your purpose and your values, then your leadership model might be running the show and it will miss the constraint of your model for living. Simply put, you will be and remain out of balance because you have not done the work to identify what balance means for you — what it actually looks like in your life.

Why here, why now?

We are not machines, we are human — and we have more than just our professional side. Whether we recognize it or not, we all have our own model for a life worth living.

At some point we will all encounter a moment, either as we grow older or as a result of a life-altering event, that causes us to pause and ask important questions:

- Why am I here?

- What is my purpose?

- What do I value?

- What does a life worth living look like to me?

- What does it look like for me to live into that life?

These are the questions that are defined in your model for living.

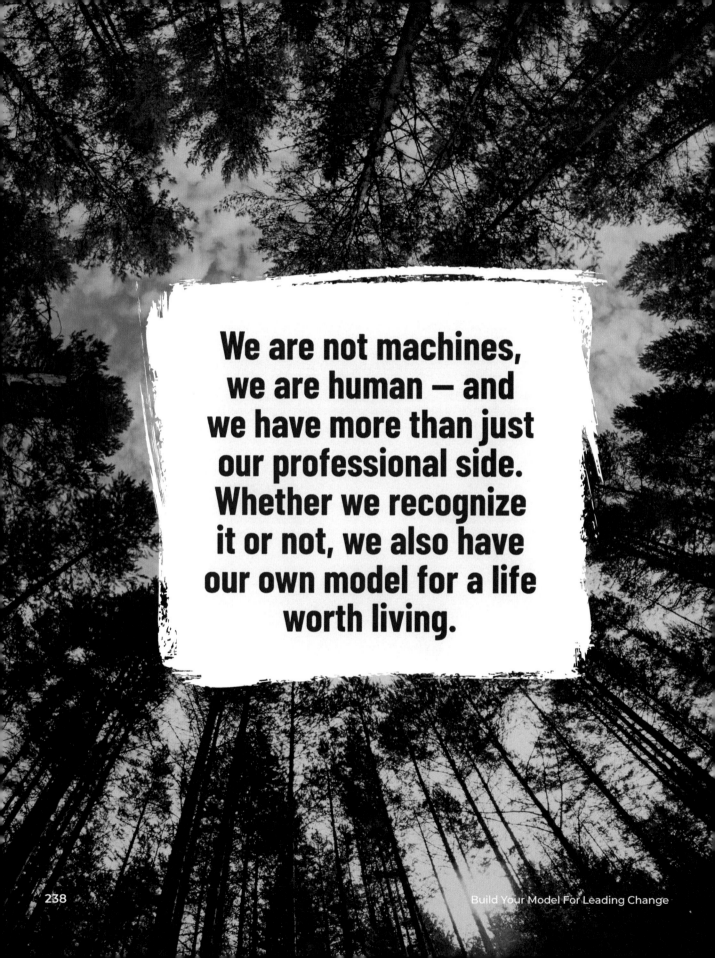

We are not machines, we are human — and we have more than just our professional side. Whether we recognize it or not, we also have our own model for a life worth living.

CRISIS MOMENTS

Breakdown to Breakthrough

The day my mom was diagnosed with Alzheimer's disease, it changed my world. I would later learn that I was part of the "sandwich generation" — those of us who find ourselves raising our own children and also becoming primary caregivers to our parents. I have always wrestled with what it looks like to have a balance between work and home. But in the 15 months from the time of that diagnosis to needing to sell my mom's house and move her in to live with my husband, daughter, and me, I would learn that I could not keep going at the same work pace without revisiting my model for living first.

At the time, I was already clear about my life purpose and values — but I hadn't yet done the work of exploring what they had to tell me about my model for living and how to balance my "life" with my "work." In other words, what I didn't have was a way to balance all the roles I was playing: wife, mom, girl scout cookie mom, CEO, coach, team coach, child turned primary caregiver for the parent, coordinator and manager of all care ... the list of roles seemed to have grown exponentially overnight.

Many of us never stop to think about creating a model for living until we are in a crisis of some sort. A moment where what has been working is no longer working. An external event like the death of a loved one, a diagnosis, a health scare, being

fired, etc. Or an internal event or epiphany where a goal that you have spent your life pursuing (a job, title, status, lottery win, new house, new car, etc.) is suddenly no longer meaningful for you. David Kantor calls these moments the origin of our "breakdown to breakthrough" stories — the moment when, looking back, we can see that everything changed in some meaningful way.

While breakdown moments can be painful and full of despair, they often serve to catalyze the kind of thinking that building your model for living calls for. Crises, in all their darkness, have the capacity to create a moment of pause. Of re-evaluation.

On the other side of these moments, we can find the gift of clarity in our values, a re-prioritization of what's important and not important, a set of principles that will be unwavering, and a model in practice that will ensure our values and principles are not only espoused but enacted in our lives.

Notably, while many of us may experience multiple breakdown-to-breakthrough stories, I don't believe you *need* to experience one to begin building your model for living! The goal of developing your model for living now — ideally when you're not in crisis — is to create a compass to guide you. Think of it as a North Star to follow when you need it most.

Chapter 5 | Your Model for Living: What Does It Mean to Live a Life Worth Living?

239

THE PERIL OF SUCCESS AND THE ENDLESS PURSUIT OF MORE

Success is a double-edged sword.

I don't think I know of anyone who wakes up every morning and rolls out of bed saying, "I want to fail today" or "I don't want to be successful." But successful leaders are often faced with a dilemma that places pressure on their leadership model and their model for living: success often generates more success, more recognition, more requests, more money, more status, more authority, more space in the market, etc. In other words, the unique dilemma of success is that success becomes circular and expansive. And when it does, we often create a narrative that says, "I have to do this," "I have no choice," or "If I don't do this then I'll lose everything."

These stories we tell ourselves become the guiding narrative for our decisions and decision-making — and they can become so strong that we even build our models around them.

Without a diligent and thoughtful practice around developing your model for living, the perils of success and the endless cycle of "more" can easily become the "breakdown moment"

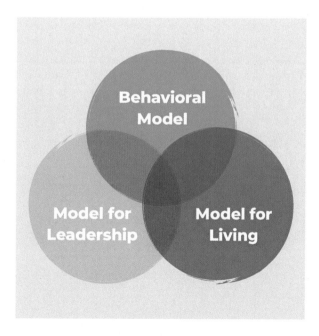

in a breakdown-to-breakthrough story — when success breeds more success and further demands on our time until one day we notice we are *waaaay* out of alignment.

ARE YOU READY?

In this section, we return to the four components of a complete model that you used in the last chapter to develop your model for leadership. But this time, you'll be guided through questions to help you define and articulate your model for living.

Take your time! The following questions will likely catalyze some deep thinking, and it's worth moving through the process thoughtfully and fully.

NOTE TO READERS: While all of the work in this workbook is personal, this section on building a model around your life's purpose and why you are here can be particularly challenging and difficult to reflect on.

This is your reminder that we all need structures and people around us who can support this kind of exploration. So, as you do this work, lean on a thinking partner or reach out to a trained professional — a certified coach, a clinical social worker, a certified therapist, or other mental health specialists. These are all wonderful guides should you want more support as you move through this section.

Model for Living:
Theory of the Thing

What are your principles for living?

This section functions as both an articulation of principles and a call to action. You can think of it as your personal manifesto. A declaration of your core values and beliefs — what you stand for and how you intend to live your life.

Reflection Time

Values represent who you are.

What are your values?

Chapter 5 | Your Model for Living: What Does It Mean to Live a Life Worth Living?

243

Reflection Time

Use the following questions to prompt further reflection:

- What brings me joy?

- What do I stand for?

- What are my strongest beliefs?

- How do I want to live my life?

- Have I been loved?

- Am I able to receive love?

- Am I able to give love?

- What are the words that reflect how I want to live my life?

Build Your Model For Leading Change

NOTES

Reflection Time

What are the principles on which you have built your life?

Examples of the kinds of reflections that might emerge for you:

- Be kind

- I am grateful for everything I have

- Joy is the key to everything

- Practicing self care is not selfish

- Words matter

- Keep learning

Remember, there are no right or wrong answers here. Just self-exploration and self-awareness. If you are being honest and clear with yourself, you are on the right track!

Build Your Model For Leading Change

My principles for living:

THE TIME DILEMMA

Who wouldn't like more time in their day?

Organizational life is busy, with one deadline stacked after the other, and there is no doubt that we collectively seem to move from crisis to crisis at a global level. Bemoaning the time warp that happens for many of us as we juggle the competing demands of work, life, and the multiple roles we each fill often becomes a point of connection we make with others. And as we are collectively coming out of the COVID pandemic and trying to determine what life will look like now, it seems there is no lack of people just moving from one meeting to the next — often with no break in between.

How do you relate to time?

A number of years ago, I vowed to break up with the word "busy" and strike it from my vocabulary. I was tired of hearing myself use it, but I also came to realize that it was a self-fulfilling prophecy. What we perceive as a "lack of time" is a major story we sometimes tell ourselves. Do not fall for that trap!

What we value and prioritize, we create time for.

This is your space to be thoughtful and intentional about your relationship with time.

- What is your relationship to time?

- Where do you create time for connection and relationships?

- Where do you create time to go slow?

- What reflective practices do you incorporate into your life?

- Where do you go fast in life? How do you focus in these moments of speed?

NOTES

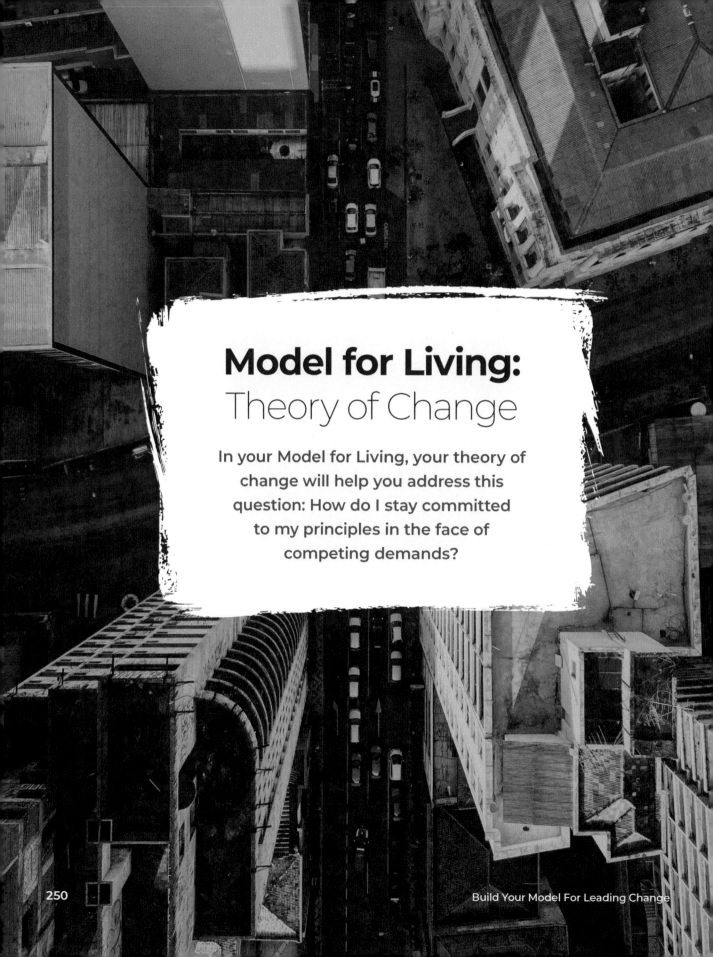

Model for Living:
Theory of Change

In your Model for Living, your theory of change will help you address this question: How do I stay committed to my principles in the face of competing demands?

Remember the example I offered earlier about the leader whose model for living contained a value and principle of "dedicated family time" but who felt so completely stepped on by the constant demands of his team that eventually he lost control, lashed out at his boss, and lost his job? Well, his example is a perfect case of a model for living being constrained by a model for leadership. In his case, his leadership model included an "open door policy" for his team. But when there was a crisis in the organization, it resulted in his team reaching out to him at all hours of the day to talk about challenges they were experiencing.

While his intentions were good and he wanted to be supportive of the team, the situation had resulted in an overemphasis of his model for leadership and sent him flying out of alignment with his model for living. In this example, the story could have ended much differently if he had a clear theory of change — a vision for how he could find better alignment when we realized his models were in conflict.

For example, if he had asked, "How do I stay committed to my principles in the face of competing demands?" he might have decided to revisit his model for living for insight into how he could more effectively constrain his leadership model. He might have reflected again on his values and principles and re-committed to setting boundaries for when he would respond to his team. For example, he might have made a plan to communicate new boundaries to his team that emphasized his desire to remain highly supportive while enacting more effective constraints around "when."

What is the interaction between your model for living and your model for leading (or any of your professional models)? As my own example above illustrates, they will support and constrain each other.

Now it's your turn. Ready to explore how your models are interacting?

Chapter 5 | Your Model for Living: What Does It Mean to Live a Life Worth Living?

251

Grab A Pen!

On the following page draw a circle that proportionally represents your model for leadership. The size and location should represent how much attention and focus it's getting right now.

Next, draw a circle for your model for living, as it relates to your model for leadership. The size and location should represent how much attention and focus it's getting right now.

Now that you've drawn your circles, explore the following questions:

What would "balance" between these models look like for me? How would I know?

What implications do I see in the gaps that exist between my behavioral model, my model for living, and my leadership model?

What, if anything, do I want to change?

What would be helpful in supporting this change?

Model for Living:
Theory of Practice

Your theory of practice when it comes to
your model for living clearly states the actions
you intend to take that will convey your
principles to the world.

Taking Inventory

List the values and principles you identified in the section above in the Theory of the "Thing."

For each one, rate it on a scale of 1 to 10 — how true are your actions to this principle today?

Value/Principle	How true to this value/principle are you being today? Scale 1–10 1: not true 10: completely true	How true would you like it to be 6 months from now?

Chapter 5 | Your Model for Living: What Does It Mean to Live a Life Worth Living?

255

Reflection Time

Using your principles and ratings above, reflect on the following questions:

What will you start doing now?

What will you stop doing?

What will you say "no" to in the future?

NOTES

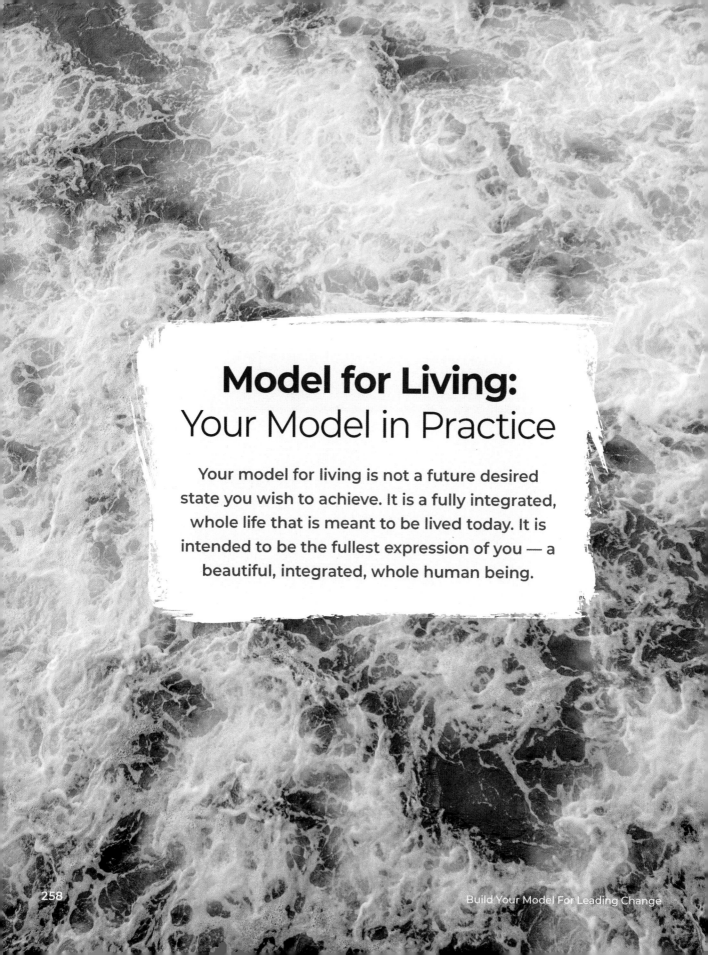

Model for Living:
Your Model in Practice

Your model for living is not a future desired state you wish to achieve. It is a fully integrated, whole life that is meant to be lived today. It is intended to be the fullest expression of you — a beautiful, integrated, whole human being.

A PERSONAL JOURNEY WITH MY MODEL FOR LIVING

This past January I took a month off. Not to travel, or visit friends, or write a book, or work on any of the various ideas that float around in my head all day bringing me energy and joy. Nope, the month off was simply to be with myself and my family and work on my model for living. I've learned that while I can get very excited about lots of ideas and taking action on them, I often do this at the expense of my own personal health.

Intellectually, I know that a solid night's sleep, movement and exercise, eating well (really well), and finding white space in my day to journal, reflect, and meditate are all essential to my well-being. They are not optional, and yet I was making them expendable, and in turn sacrificing my well-being and health.

At the end of last year, I looked up and realized just how much of a gap existed between what I espouse as my values for living and what was really happening. My models looked a little like the diagram below, with the professional side (my leadership model) overtaking the living side of my life.

My intentions for creating practices for my self-care had encountered the enemy: many competing demands during COVID had overtaken almost all of my daily activities.

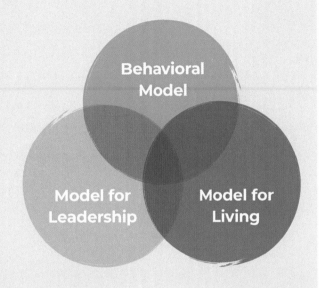

The result was that I was out of integrity with the principles in my model for living.

So I took a month off and set about to put structures in place to help me stay more balanced this year. It's going well, and as I write this I'm aware that I've made some choices recently that are impacting my life. But I'm getting more skillful at noticing this before it takes over. I'm clear about this being a moment in time. It will not last past the next two weeks, and while the professional side is dominating a bit, it's not at the expense of health and well-being.

As my story in the call-out box shows, it's one thing to know your values (your theory of the thing). It's another thing altogether to have a clear sense of how you will maintain a commitment to your values in relation to your model for leadership and your behavioral model (this is your theory of change). But what my story shows more than anything else is how important it is to have a process that allows you to periodically check in with yourself to recognize when you are living in integrity with your model for living and when you are outside your principles.

This is the feedback loop that comes from having a theory of practice and a commitment to checking in to see if it's in alignment with your model in practice.

BUILDING IN A FEEDBACK LOOP

In my life, I have a habit of losing my alignment when I am being my most creative self. In structural terms, it takes the form of Move, Random, Power.

I might be working on a creative project that I value, but in my excitement and creativity, I can sometimes lose myself. I deprioritize reflection and journaling time. I give up exercise time and replace it with work tasks. I am better about catching these moments now than I used to be, and I'm better at taking action to change them — when I catch sight of them. But it is because I have built a feedback loop that helps me catch sight and course correct that I can trust in my creative process and know that I'm still in alignment with my model for living.

So, what does this feedback loop look like? For me, my feedback loop includes intentionally creating space where I will let my creative vision take over, and then taking strategic pauses — reset moments — where I will get back in alignment with what I know makes me feel fulfilled, alive, and grateful.

During my reset moments, I ask:

- What is the story I am making up about time and the lack of time for self?
- What is this story costing me?
- What's at risk if I continue on this path?
- Is the current journey worth the risk?
- If yes, what's the boundary? And how will I know when I'm there?
- If no, what's the new story I want to tell myself about time? What will be important to me now?
- Where will I take action to recommit to myself?
- What do I need to support myself as I make this re-commitment?

What might an effective feedback loop look like for you?

Here are some questions to consider:

- How can you build in a regular practice of checking in with yourself about whether you are living and working in alignment with both your model for living and your leadership model?
- What kinds of questions might you ask yourself during your "reset moment"?

Reflection Time

Reflect on this quote:

"Our deepest fear is not that we are inadequate. Our deepest fear is that we are powerful beyond measure. It is our light, not our darkness that most frightens us. We ask ourselves, 'Who am I to be brilliant, gorgeous, talented, fabulous?' Actually, who are you not to be? You are a child of God. Your playing small does not serve the world. There is nothing enlightened about shrinking so that other people won't feel insecure around you. We are all meant to shine, as children do. We were born to make manifest the glory of God that is within us. It's not just in some of us; it's in everyone. And as we let our own light shine, we unconsciously give other people permission to do the same. As we are liberated from our own fear, our presence automatically liberates others."

Marianne Williamson

NOTES

Chapter 5 | Your Model for Living: What Does It Mean to Live a Life Worth Living?

263

MY MODEL FOR LIVING IN SUMMARY

Your model for living will continue to evolve over time, but here are some of the key features that you are now able to clearly articulate in relation to what a life of fullness, fulfillment, and meaning looks like for you.

Capture a summary of what you want to remember here.

My principles for living are:

In the face of competing demands, I will maintain commitment to my values by:

The practices that keep me aligned and resonant with my model for living are:

The actions I will take to put my model into practice are:

What will happen when I notice gaps between my model for living, my theory of practice, and my model in practice? How will I check in with myself?

How will I give myself grace for the gaps I find?

How will I return to my version of balance?

What will I do to hold myself accountable?

Reflection Time

Reflections on Your Model

Now that you have something on paper, journal about your experience of defining your model for living. What was it like? What was easy? What did you find more difficult?

Constraint and Gaps

All models are helpful and also have their limitations. Make note of gaps or places that you want to continue to grow or refine.

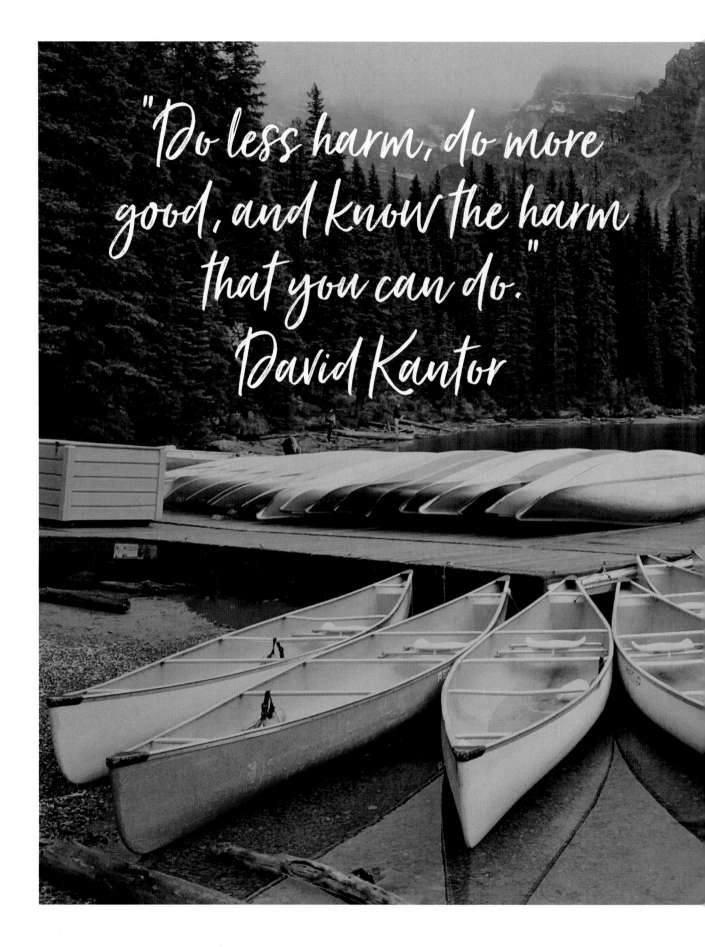

"Do less harm, do more good, and know the harm that you can do."
David Kantor

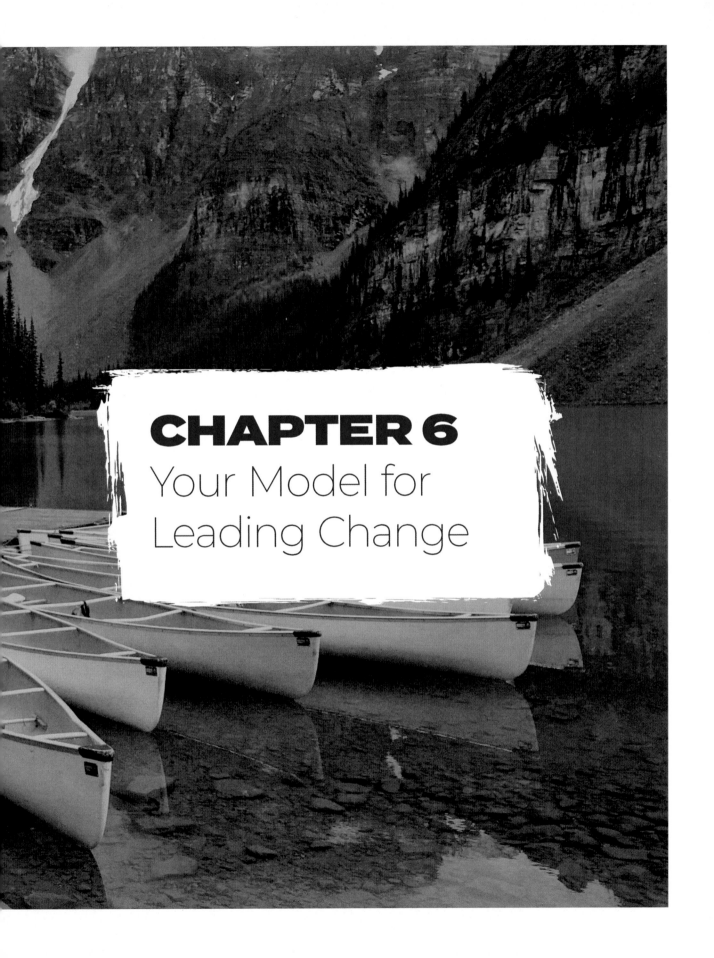

CHAPTER 6
Your Model for
Leading Change

The work you've done in this workbook has laid a deep foundation of functional self-awareness. You are now familiar with your behavioral model, you have a sense of what leadership looks like for you as well as how you think about growing and developing leadership in yourself and others, and you have a model for living that will help you stay clear about what balance looks like for you when it comes to work life and home life.

This thinking sets you up to continue your model-building journey. Indeed, these three primary models — your behavioral model, your leadership model, and your model for living — are the foundational models from which all other models will evolve.

These core models are your "lens" for how you see the world around you.

As I shared in the introduction, there are many models you might go on to build for yourself, including those that reflect your personal beliefs and practices and your professional needs and values.

In this final model-building chapter, you will build on all the work you have done so far to build a model for leading change.

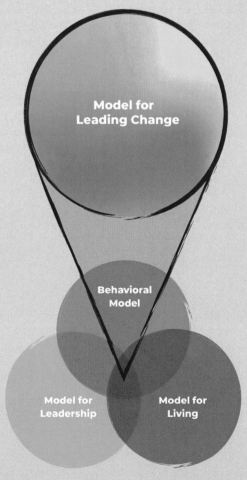

Model for
Leading Change

Behavioral
Model

Model for
Leadership

Model for
Living

Build Your Model For Leading Change

LEADER AS INTERVENTIONIST

Leadership, by its very nature, will include intervention. And we all have the opportunity, should we choose to take it on, of stepping into the role of being an interventionist — regardless of our positional role within our organizations or within the existing power hierarchy we are embedded in.

An interventionist is able to see, name, and intervene in a breakdown of communication in order to change the nature of the outcome.

Whether you are a senior leader in your organization, a team member on a small team, or an external consultant, coach, or agile coach, you can intervene when the need arises by observing and actively engaging to change established or emerging patterns of communication.

In my experience, I have found that most organizational challenges — failed transformation initiatives, crises, failures, etc. — can be traced back to failures in communication. This might look like, for example, a CEO and a COO who consistently talk past one another and leave conversations feeling frustrated and unheard. Or it might look like a crisis in an organization whose culture does not value the language of Affect in conversation — thus catalyzing a mass exodus of valued talent due to employees not feeling heard or valued by executives. It could take the form of a reorganization that results in the appointment of co-CEOs who are unable to find a way to talk and think together. It might be a large-scale transformation toward agility that is struggling to progress because the culture of the organization does not reward surfacing the real issues that are blocking the workflow. Or, it could look like an agile team who considers themselves to be high-performing but often stifles their own creativity by deferring to the voice of one senior team member rather than exploring ideas voiced by others.

In each of these instances, communication breaks down. Real issues and unexplored ideas remain "underground" — spoken about only through the subterranean communication networks where meaningful dialogue and engagement are unlikely to ever occur.

But here's the thing: it does not need to take a crisis for us to start developing our "communicative competence." Rather, it takes the willingness of individuals to step into the role of interventionist and be willing to learn how to see, name, and intervene in communication breakdowns.

This is where leading change begins — by noticing when there is an opportunity to change course, interrupt in patterns that are not serving the collective good, and help achieve a different outcome.

Do less harm, do more good, and know the harm you can do

Because the role of an interventionist includes the ability to shift and change the nature of the outcome, it can lead to transformational and sustainable change. But the role is not without challenge.

According to David Kantor, an effective oath for an interventionist should be, "Do less harm, do more good, and know the harm that you can do." This oath is slightly different from the Hippocratic Oath for doctors mandating that they "do no harm." What Kantor understood well is that, by our very nature and based on the webs of visible and invisible realities that influence why we do what we do, it would be nearly impossible for us to do no harm. This is why he advocated for the ongoing practice of developing our own functional self-awareness and the ability to "bystand on ourselves" in the moment.

Becoming an effective interventionist means owning and taking responsibility for the ways in which our behavioral model will impact how we lead change and knowing the areas that may challenge us. For me, this looks like being careful of my relationship to the voice of Oppose, recognizing that it can trigger me. This awareness is particularly important when I'm working with teams, as I also value and believe in the role that the voice of opposition plays in team development and overall change. By knowing the harm I can do — and taking ownership and responsibility for my actions when triggered — I am able to work with and through challenging moments in a way that lets me do less harm and more good when I'm in the room with teams.

Reflection Time

React to this oath:
"Do less harm, do more good, and know the harm you can do."

- What does this oath mean to you?

- What about this idea challenges you?

- What is important to you about this oath?

- What aspects of this statement would you keep, change, discard, or invent in your own model for leading change?

Exploring Your Metaphor for Change

Note: while you can do this exercise on your own, it will be most impactful when done alongside a thinking partner.

Whether we are aware of it or not, we all likely have a metaphor for change. Common metaphors include:

- The metamorphosis of a caterpillar into a butterfly (i.e., total transformation)

- A rocketship taking flight (i.e., linear and rapid upward progress)

- The changing of the seasons (i.e., ongoing and gradual evolution)

1. What is your metaphor for how change happens?

Individually reflect on this question and then draw or write out the story of your metaphor.

> Change is like...

2. Share your metaphor with your thinking partner. Describe it in vivid detail to them.

3. Ask your thinking partner to help you explore the following questions:

- What is your role in this change?

- What kind of energy does this role create for you?

- How does change happen?

- What makes change successful?

- What factors contribute to unsuccessful change?

- What is a belief that you are holding on to tightly about change?

EXERCISE

4. Refer back to your Heroic Modes (Chapter 2, Juncture 4): Fixer, Protector, Survivor. What, if any, of these heroic themes show up in your metaphor for change?

5. Ask your thinking partner to reflect back to you the themes they heard. Capture your notes here:

6. Now, switch roles and conduct the same conversation with your thinking partner. What, if anything, did they share that you might want to borrow in your own thinking about change?

EXPLORING THEORIES OF CHANGE

There are numerous theories of change and how change happens.

For an in-depth exploration of change, review any text on Organization Development — the field of study that looks at the practices, systems, techniques, and mindset that affect organizational change.

Bob Marshak (2010) offers a high-level summary of how the theories of organizational change have evolved over time, from thinking about organizations as mechanical systems that may be "broken" and need to be "fixed" to more current thinking that views organizations as complex, emergent entities that are socially constructed through conversation and language.

In the chart below, I've offered a brief summary of these theories as they have evolved through the lens of specific fields of inquiry.

	Diagnostic Organization Development: 1940s – Present		Dialogic Organization Development: 1980s – Present	
Field of inquiry	Mechanical Sciences (1900s–)	Biological Sciences (1960s -)	Interpretive Sciences (1980s–)	Complexity Sciences (1990s–)
Organizations are:	Determinate, closed systems	Contingent, open systems	Generative, meaning-making systems	Complex, adaptive systems
Focus is on:	Efficiency, plans, structure, productivity	Alignment, adaptation, congruence, fit	Discourse, meaning, culture, consciousness	Self-organization, emergent design
Change happens by:	Fixing and re-engineering	Adapting and repositioning	Reframing and renaming	Flux and emergence

Reflection Time

Using your metaphor for change, reflect on which theories your metaphor aligns with or incorporates.

Model-Building Reflections:
LEADING CHANGE

Reflect back on your Inventory of Models in Chapter 3.

- Which of these models are models for change?

- Which models would you bring forward to Imitate or Constrain in your model for change?

- What is something you would invent in your model for change?

Make notes about what you would keep, re-shape, discard, and invent in your model based on your reflections of the initial inventory you made in Chapter 3.

TOPIC / MODEL: LEADING CHANGE

Keep

Re-Shape

Discard

Invent

Model for Leading Change:
The Components

The components of your model for leading change, just like your leadership model, will include articulating the following:

- **The theory of the "thing"** — What's the focus or subject of your model?

- **The theory of change** — How do you believe that change is brought about within or for the "thing" that you are focusing on?

- **The theory of practice** — What do you believe about what you should do, based on your understanding of the "thing" and how it changes?

- **The model in practice** - What do you actually do "in the room" to make change happen?

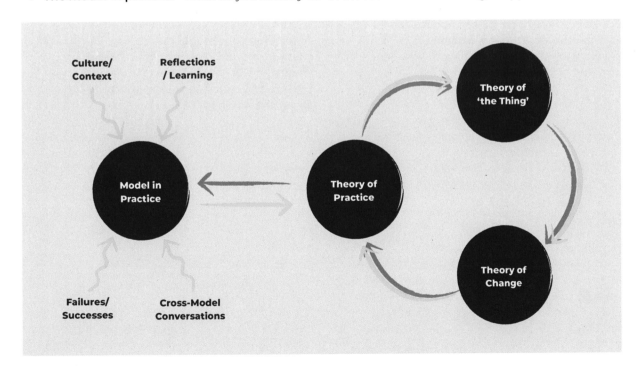

Model for Leading Change:
Theory of the Thing

We use the word "change" to mean many things in reference to different contexts.

- How do I get other people to change?
- How do I get my organization to change?
- How do I get my team to do something differently?

The word *change* often signals that we are seeking a future that is different from our current reality.

But being able to create change means being able to articulate what — specifically — you are wanting to change, and what your role is in bringing about that change.

If your role is an Executive Leader and you want to bring about change for your organization, then the "thing" in your model for leading change may be "organizations" (i.e., leading change for organizations). The next step would be to explore your "theory of change" and how you believe organizations change.

If your role is an Agile Team Coach and you are wanting to bring about change by helping teams become high-performing agile teams, then the "thing" in your model for leading change may be "an agile team" (i.e., leading change for an agile team). The next step would be to explore your "theory of change" and how you believe change happens for individuals and teams.

If your role is an Executive Coach and you want to bring about change by helping executives, then the "thing" in your model for leading change may be "executive leadership" (i.e., leading change for executive leadership). The next step would be to explore your "theory of change" and how you believe change happens for leaders in executive roles.

To develop your model for leading change, your first job is to identify the "thing" at the heart of what you want to change and examine your role in bringing about that change.

It's highly possible that you may have multiple models for leading change, especially if you are trying to impact change in multiple or different contexts. For example, wanting to change a process requires a different model for leading change than wanting to impact mindset or cultivate behavioral change in an organization. Personally, I have a model for how I coach executives and a separate model for how I coach leadership teams.

The point here is to start developing a model (or models) for leading change that is specific to the context in which you are trying to enact change.

Deepening Insights

What is the entity that your model for leading change is focused on?

What do you believe are the critical aspects of leading change?

What do you believe are the principles that define change done well?

What examples or experiences have shaped how you think about leading change?

Model for Leading Change:
Theory of Change

The theory of change in your model for leading change helps you clearly identify where, exactly, you are expecting to see change and how, exactly, you expect it to emerge.

Think about the complexity at the heart of what it is you are trying to change. Are there aspects of this change that are linked to or dependent on other things changing? Sometimes the change we are looking for has a straightforward cause and effect. Sometimes there are many micro-changes that set the preconditions for the change you are hoping to see.

No two changes are ever the exact same, so the processes that bring change about will look different, too. For example, if you are wanting to install a new accounting system process, that change and your process for leading it will be very different from a leader who desires to create more agility across the business.

Use the following questions to explore your theory of how change happens.

- How does change happen in relation to the "thing" that your model for leading change focuses on?

- How can change be sustained?

- What are the conditions, if any, that are necessary for change?

- Do you take a systemic view of change (as opposed to an individual view of change)? Why or why not?

- In what ways does your behavioral model (Chapter 2) and your model for leadership (Chapter 4) inform how you think about change?

NOTES

Model for Leading Change:
Theory of Practice

In this section, you're going to explore the action(s) you anticipate taking in order to lead change.

Through the following questions, you will be connecting your understanding of the "thing" at stake in your model and your understanding of how change happens in relation to the "thing." By making this connection, you will be articulating your "theory of practice" — what you believe you should be doing to lead the change you want to achieve.

Reflection Time

GOALS

- What is your focus? What is it you are trying to change?

- Reflecting on your theory of what effective change looks like, how would you go about engaging with this change process?

- What goals do you have for this process or its outcome?

GETTING STARTED

- How would you "start" the change? How do you anticipate entering into the process? What factors do you anticipate being important to the process of getting started?

- What are the prerequisites required for change to happen?

- What is your role in the change?

PRACTICES

- What are the specific practices or actions you believe you should take in order to lead the change process? Do you think these practices and actions will need to evolve over the life of the change?

- What are your boundaries in leading change? Are you part of the system or on the outside of the system?

- What role does context play in your theory of practice? Would change look different or similar in another context?

- When do you believe you should proceed with change? Under what conditions would you pause or stop the process?

PRINCIPLES

- What are the principles that are important to you to uphold while leading change?

TOOLS

- What specific tools, techniques, models, or practices do you expect to employ in leading change?

NOTES

NOTES

Model for Leading Change: Your Model in Practice

Your "model in practice" for leading change is the most visible and accessible part of your model. It's what you actually do, not just what you say you will do.

It is not unusual to experience some misalignment between your theory of change, your theory of practice, and your model in practice. This is why this final component of your model for leading change is so important. It's your opportunity to observe when and where misalignment might be showing up, note what impact it's having on your ability to lead change, and explore what you might think about differently or do differently moving forward.

Remember: your model in practice is a critical part of your feedback loop. It is where theory meets reality, offering you the opportunity to reflect, learn, and adjust as you go.

Reflection Time

- On the level of practices and behaviors, what are you choosing in the moment, and why? *Spend some time here connecting your theories with your practice: what gaps are you aware of?*

- Where do you change, adapt, or abandon your theory of practice in your actual practice? What leads you to make the adaptation?

- Where does your model for leadership influence or impact your model in practice for leading change?

- Where does your behavioral model support your model in practice for leading change? Where does it give you trouble?

NOTES

NOTES

DELVING DEEPER INTO YOUR FEEDBACK LOOP

One of the most impactful ways to help you align your "theory of practice" with your "model in practice" for leading change is to solicit outside feedback. Doing so can bring new insights, deepen your awareness, and help you see blindspots that you might not otherwise be attuned to.

But, a word of caution about feedback! Be careful not to ask for feedback about yourself and how people might like — or not like — your actions. **The work of change is not about being liked. It is about impact and effectiveness.**

The feedback you ask for should be focused on questions like:

- Are we talking about the right things?

- What change is happening?

- What is the evidence for the change?

- Did we learn something?

- Are we evolving?

The following prompts are designed to help you prepare to receive productive feedback — both about your change leadership and the model for leading change that you are developing. As part of this ongoing process, I also encourage you to further reflect on what you discover through the reflective journaling process described in this book's introduction.

PREPARING TO RECEIVE FEEDBACK

Preparing to ask for — and receive — effective and productive feedback can feel vulnerable. It can also feel vulnerable to give honest feedback when asked for it. So the goal here is to think critically about how to set yourself and your team up for success.

What structures will you put in place to enable feedback about the effectiveness and sustainability of the change you are leading?

What is your goal in receiving feedback?

CONSTRAINT AND GAPS

All models are helpful, and they all have their limitations. The goal here is to set yourself up to receive useful feedback regarding how well your model for leading change is supporting you and your process.

1 Share your model with a thinking partner. Ask them to offer constraint in the form of questions they might have about your model. Ask them to explore with you to discover gaps or areas that may need more thought in your evolving model for leading change.

2 What gaps, if any, are illuminated by this conversation in regards to your theory of the "thing," your theory of change, your theory of practice, and your model in practice?

3 Make note of where you see a "growth edge" — gaps or places that you want to continue to grow or refine in your model and your practice.

NOTES

MY MODEL FOR LEADING CHANGE IN SUMMARY

Model building is ongoing work. You will continue to refine your model for leading change over time, but here are some of the key features that you are now able to clearly articulate when leading change for yourself and others.

Capture a summary of what you want to remember here.

When leading change, I focus on...

I believe change happens by...

Positionally, my role in leading change is to...

I take the following actions...

My growth edge is...

NOTES

NOTES

We're all getting ready...

to be ready for something.

CHAPTER 7
Where to from here?

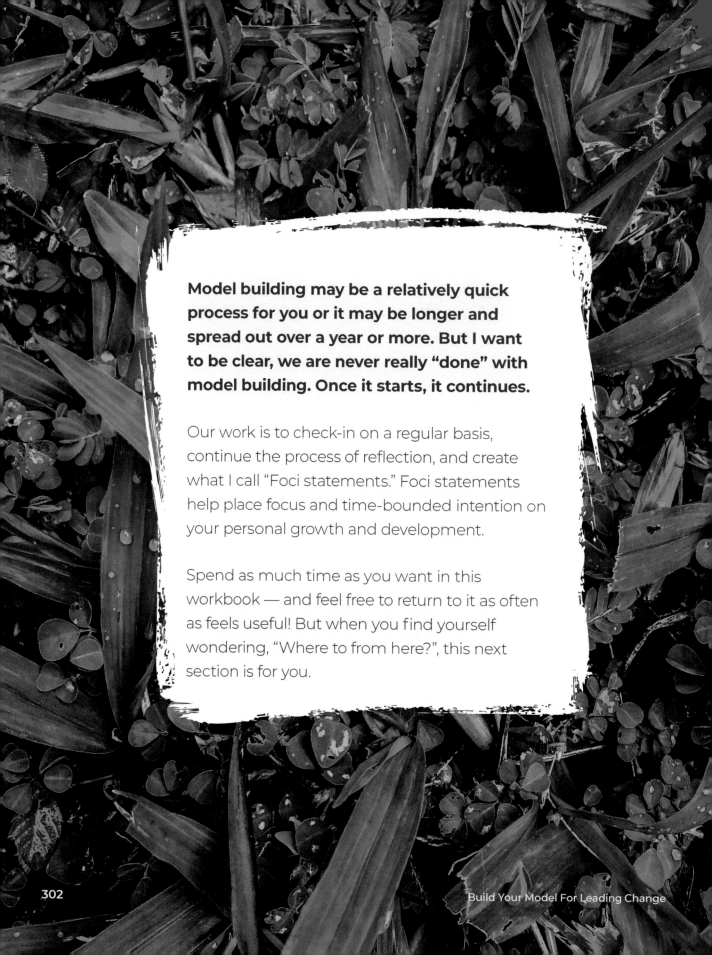

Model building may be a relatively quick process for you or it may be longer and spread out over a year or more. But I want to be clear, we are never really "done" with model building. Once it starts, it continues.

Our work is to check-in on a regular basis, continue the process of reflection, and create what I call "Foci statements." Foci statements help place focus and time-bounded intention on your personal growth and development.

Spend as much time as you want in this workbook — and feel free to return to it as often as feels useful! But when you find yourself wondering, "Where to from here?", this next section is for you.

CREATING YOUR FOCI STATEMENTS

Many of us are used to setting goals, often formatted as an objective and key result. These are typically created in the form of an outcome you desire.

For example, my objective may be to improve my leadership, and I could define key results like 1) get a promotion, 2) attend the leadership cohort program, and 3) see 15% improvement on my leadership effectiveness score in my next 360.

But in the space of personal growth, I would challenge the idea that you know ahead of time exactly what you will get when you aim for "improved leadership." And what you think will work today will most certainly change in two months when you get a new boss, or the company announces a downsize, or the market takes an unprecedented dive. Any and all of these circumstances would require you to adapt and change.

Goals serve an important function in organizations and when working with team members — you don't need to discard them! But when it comes to personal growth and focusing on our behavior, I'm going to ask you to try something new: creating a Foci statement.

What are they?

Foci statements are futuristic statements about who you want to be as a leader (whether it's as a coach, team coach, interventionist, parent, spouse, etc.). These statements are set in the future, ideally 6–9 months from today, and they are stated in a positive manner as if what they state were true right now.

Foci statements are intended to help you close gaps you identify in your behavioral model or leadership model. A good Foci statement should stretch you. It might even make you itchy to write it down, and that's a good thing.

Foci statements become your compass or guiding north star.

Here's why: my theory of how change happens for humans is that it starts with being clear about where we are going.

Foci statements are affirmations of the way you want to be. And they read as though they have already been achieved. For example:

"I am a courageous and authentic leader."

A Foci statement is a stretch — an aspiration. It will feel like it's something that you are longing for but that you have possibly created a story around that says you can't have it or that it's not fully attainable.

What's my focus?

Think back to the work you've been doing in this workbook on your behavioral model and your model for leadership.

- What's an area you want to focus on in your behavioral model?

- What gaps do you notice between your theory of leadership and how you show up in your profession each day?

- Given all of this, if you could be anything, what would you desire to be right now?

Brainstorm the ideas that come to mind...

Of the things you desire to be, which ones already feel true? List them here:

Of the things you desire to be, which ones feel like a stretch? List them here:

The stretch statements and the take-your-breath-away statements are the ones to focus on! Take these ideas and work on crafting them into foci statements.

Creating your Foci statements

What are 2–4 Foci statements you would like to set for the next 6 months to help you focus on deepening your awareness of self, your leadership, or cultivating your life worth living?

Putting concept into practice...

A leader I worked with was strong in the action of Follow and placed a heavy emphasis on getting things done, particularly if it would benefit the company and help to gain market share immediately.

The impact he was having on others is that they saw him as robotic and compliant. They saw him as taking suggestions from key contributors at face value and de-emphasizing the voices and concerns of others. A few team members had come to believe that he didn't care about anyone else but the key players, and they felt their opinions were marginalized and devalued. They had stopped actively participating in meetings.

After receiving some feedback about his impact, this leader set about to change how he was showing up in his leadership. This is one of the Foci statements he created:

I am an engaging and thoughtful leader.

He realized that he paid too much attention to a few key players because he didn't trust his knowledge in the area. He was concerned about making a mistake that could delay getting the product to market. He also realized he had been holding back on expressing some concerns about the direction the organization was heading. It was starting to concern him so much that he was losing sleep at night, but he was scared to say what he really thought in meetings.

So he developed his Foci statement and envisioned himself in it.

I am an engaging and thoughtful leader.

- When I don't know something, I say so, every time

- I actively invite other opinions into conversations from people who are quiet

- When I disagree with something, I find a way to bring my voice into the room and offer a clear Oppose

- I carve out 3 hours every other week on my calendar and schedule 1:1 calls to connect personally with each co-worker

- I actively acknowledge the things I appreciate about my co-workers on a regular basis

- I receive unsolicited feedback within 90 days that I'm having a positive impact on my colleagues and their ability to get their work done

Characteristics of a good Foci statement:

- It starts with "I am…"

- It uses present tense (as if it were already true)

- It is stated it in the positive, affirming what you want (not what you don't want)

- It is brief

- It is specific

- It includes at least one dynamic emotion or feeling word (e.g., masterful, skillful, courageous, mindful, impactful, etc.)

EXERCISE

Creating Foci statements

Step 1: Create your Foci statement. Be sure to capture 2–4 pieces of evidence, ideally with specific measures that will help you know that you are making the Foci statement come true.

Step 2: After you define your Foci statement, give it a rating in the left-hand columns using the rating scale below:

- On a scale of 1 to 10, with 1 being "not true at all" and 10 being "absolutely true," how true would you say your Foci statement is today?

- What is your desired rating in 6 months?

Foci statement 1

	Rating Today	Desired Rating

Foci statement 2

	Rating Today	Desired Rating

EXERCISE

Foci statement 3

	Rating Today	Desired Rating

Foci statement 4

	Rating Today	Desired Rating

MONTHLY REFLECTIONS

Revisit your workbook monthly and use this structure to support you in noticing and reflecting on your behavioral model, your leadership model, your model for living, and your model for leading change.

"Little by little, progress adds up"
Laura Casey

CHECKING IN AND LETTING GO...

At this moment, I am feeling ....

The thing that is most weighing on me at the moment is

....

Capture the worries, stresses, and to do's that are weighing on your mind.

PROGRESS IS IN THE MESS

Letting go in order to *Let Come....*

I am hopeful that ....

I am grateful for ....

CELEBRATIONS	CHALLENGES	BYSTAND	GROWTH EDGE
Something I want to celebrate is...	Something that challenged or stretched me was...	Something that I'm noticing about myself is....	What I'm working on next is...

Foci Statement Check-In

Turn back to your foci statements. Capture your reflections about where you are in relation to those intentions right now.

In this next month I want to ....

My focus or word for this coming month is:

CHECKING IN AND LETTING GO...

At this moment, I am feeling ....

The thing that is most weighing on me at the moment is

....

Capture the worries, stresses, and to do's that are weighing on your mind.

PROGRESS IS IN THE MESS

Letting go in order to *Let Come....*

I am hopeful that ....

I am grateful for ....

CELEBRATIONS	CHALLENGES	BYSTAND	GROWTH EDGE
Something I want to celebrate is...	Something that challenged or stretched me was...	Something that I'm noticing about myself is....	What I'm working on next is...

Foci Statement Check-In

Turn back to your foci statements. Capture your reflections about where you are in relation to those intentions right now.

In this next month I want to ....

My focus or word for this coming month is:

CHECKING IN AND LETTING GO...

At this moment, I am feeling ....

The thing that is most weighing on me at the moment is

....

Capture the worries, stresses, and to do's that are weighing on your mind.

PROGRESS IS IN THE MESS

Letting go in order to *Let Come....*

I am hopeful that ....

I am grateful for ....

CELEBRATIONS	CHALLENGES	BYSTAND	GROWTH EDGE
Something I want to celebrate is...	Something that challenged or stretched me was...	Something that I'm noticing about myself is....	What I'm working on next is...

Foci Statement Check-In

Turn back to your foci statements. Capture your reflections about where you are in relation to those intentions right now.

Build Your Model For Leading Change

In this next month I want to ....

My focus or word for this coming month is:

CHECKING IN AND LETTING GO...

At this moment, I am feeling ....

The thing that is most weighing on me at the moment is

....

Capture the worries, stresses, and to do's that are weighing on your mind.

PROGRESS IS IN THE MESS

Letting go in order to *Let Come....*

I am hopeful that ....

I am grateful for ....

CELEBRATIONS	CHALLENGES	BYSTAND	GROWTH EDGE
Something I want to celebrate is...	Something that challenged or stretched me was...	Something that I'm noticing about myself is....	What I'm working on next is...

Foci Statement Check-In

Turn back to your foci statements. Capture your reflections about where you are in relation to those intentions right now.

In this next month I want to ....

My focus or word for this coming month is:

CHECKING IN AND LETTING GO...

At this moment, I am feeling ....

The thing that is most weighing on me at the moment is

....

Capture the worries, stresses, and to do's that are weighing on your mind.

PROGRESS IS IN THE MESS

Letting go in order to *Let Come....*

I am hopeful that ....

I am grateful for ....

CELEBRATIONS	CHALLENGES	BYSTAND	GROWTH EDGE
Something I want to celebrate is...	Something that challenged or stretched me was...	Something that I'm noticing about myself is....	What I'm working on next is...

Foci Statement Check-In

Turn back to your foci statements. Capture your reflections about where you are in relation to those intentions right now.

Build Your Model For Leading Change

In this next month I want to ....

My focus or word for this coming month is:

CHECKING IN AND LETTING GO...

At this moment, I am feeling ....

The thing that is most weighing on me at the moment is

....

Capture the worries, stresses, and to do's that are weighing on your mind.

PROGRESS IS IN THE MESS

Letting go in order to *Let Come....*

I am hopeful that ....

I am grateful for ....

CELEBRATIONS	CHALLENGES	BYSTAND	GROWTH EDGE
Something I want to celebrate is...	Something that challenged or stretched me was...	Something that I'm noticing about myself is....	What I'm working on next is...

Foci Statement Check-In

Turn back to your foci statements. Capture your reflections about where you are in relation to those intentions right now.

In this next month I want to ....

My focus or word for this coming month is:

Build Your Model For Leading Change

NOTES

NOTES

REFERENCES

Donald Schon, *The Reflective Practitioner: How Professionals Think in Action* (Routledge, 1992).

David Kantor, *Reading the Room: Group Dynamics for Coaches and Leaders* (Jossey-Bass, 2012).

David Kantor, *Becoming an Interventionist* (Independently Published, 2019).

Grady McGonagill, *"Reflections on Practice Through Model Building: One Person's Experience," Reflections: The SoL North America Journal on Knowledge, Learning, and Change 14: No. 2* (2014), 1–22.

Grady McGonagill, *"Annotated Bibliography on Leadership"* (available online).

Robert (Bob) Marshak, *"OD Morphogenesis: The emerging dialgoic platform of premises. Practicing Social Change, 1 (2)* (2010), 4-9.

Sarah Hill, *Where Did You Learn To Behave Like That?: A Coaching Guide For Working With Leaders* (Dialogix, 2017).

Sarah Hill and Tony Melville, *Model Building for Leaders and Coaches* (Dialogix, 2019).

NOTES

A FINAL SEND-OFF...

Regardless of where you are on your model-building journey, you are right where you are meant to be.

The process of model building can be part of your life's work, should you choose to undertake the task. It can be a never done, always evolving process of becoming clearer about your thinking and why you do what you do.

Or, it can be a moment in time. You may have completed this thinking journey in record time and be completely satisfied with where you are and enjoying the enhanced clarity you have for yourself and those you work with. That's okay too!

There is no deadline. If you paused in the middle of this book or became overwhelmed, be patient with yourself. Put it aside, and when you're ready for it, the work will find you. You don't need to make it happen.

We're all just getting ready to be ready for something.

Keep growing your leadership range and building your model for leadership. You've got this.

For more resources visit buildyourmodel.com

Made in the USA
Monee, IL
16 February 2023

27327815R00200